The Position of Woman in Primitive Society

The Position of Woman in Primitive Society

A Study of the Matriarchy

C Gasquoine Hartley
(Mrs Walter M Gallichan)

Nine
BOOKS

वाणी प्रकाशन

Presents

BOOKS

4695, 21-A, Daryaganj, New Delhi 110 002

—— Branch ——

Ashok Rajpath, Patna 800 004

Phone : +91 11 23273167 Fax : +91 11 23275710

www.vaniprakashan.in
sales@vaniprakashan.in
vaniprakashan@gmail.com

THE POSITION OF WOMAN IN PRIMITIVE SOCIETY
A STUDY OF THE MATRIARCHY
by C Gasquoine Hartley
(Mrs Walter M Gallichan)

ISBN: 978-93-5000-948-2
Feminism

First Edition

Price : ₹ 395

Printed at Printland Digital, New Delhi-110 020

Vani Prakashan's signature motif is created by Artist Maqbool Fida Husain

DEDICATION

To All Women

Be not ashamed, women, your privilege includes the rest....
You are the gates of the body, you are the gates of the soul....
And I say it is as great to be a woman as to be a man.
And I say there is nothing greater than the mother of men.

Walt Whitman
7 Carlton Terrace,
Child's Hill

Contents

The Primitive Family

Introductory

THE TWENTIETH CENTURY is the Age of Woman; some day, it may be that it will be looked back upon as the golden age, the dawn, some say, of feminine civilisation. We cannot estimate as yet; and no man can tell what forces these new conditions may not release in the soul of woman. The modern change is that the will of woman is asserting itself. Women are looking for a satisfactory life, which is to be determined from within themselves, not from without by others. The result is a discontent that may well prove to be the seed or spring of further changes in a society which has yet to find its normal organisation. Yes, women are finding themselves, and men are discovering what women mean.

In the present time we are passing through a difficult period of transition. There are conditions of change that have to be met, the outcome of which it is very difficult to appreciate. A transformation in the thought and conduct of women, for which the term "revolution" is not too strong, is taking place around us; doubtless many experimental phases will be tried before we reach a new position of equilibrium.

This must be. There can be no life without movement.

The expression, "a transition period," is, of course, only relative. We often say: This or that is a sign of the present era; and, nine times out of ten, the thing we believe to be new is in reality as old as the world itself. In one sense the whole of history is a vast transition. No period stands alone; the present is in every age merely the shifting point at which the past and the future meet. All things move onwards. But the movement sometimes takes the form of a cataract, at others of an even and almost imperceptible current. This is really another way of saying that the usually slow and gradual course of change is, at certain stages, interrupted by a more or less prolonged period of revolution. The process of growth, from being gradual and imperceptible, becomes violent and conscious.

There can be little doubt that what is called the "Woman's Movement," with its disintegrating influences on social opinion and practice, is bringing vast and momentous changes in women's attitude towards the universe and towards themselves. A great motive and an enlarging ideal, a quickening of the woman's spirit, a stirring dream of a new order — these are what we have gained. We are carried on, though as yet we know not whither, and there is, of necessity, a little stumbling of our feet as we seek for a way. Hence the fear, always tending to arise in periods of social reconstruction, which is felt by many today as women pass out far beyond the established boundaries prescribed for their sex.

Whoever reflects soberly on the past history of women will not be surprised at their present movement towards emancipation. Women are reclaiming a position that is theirs by natural right — a position which once they held. It may be all very well for those who accept the authority and headship of the man as the foundation of the family and of society, to be filled with bewildered fear at what seems to them to be a quite new assertion of rights on the part of the mothers of the race. But has the family at all stages of growth been founded on the authority of the father? Our decision on this question will affect our outlook on the whole question of Woman's Rights and the relationships of the two sexes. There are civilisations, older and, as I believe, wiser than ours that have accepted the predominant position of the mother as the great central fact on which the family has been established.

The view that the family, much as it existed among the Hebrew patriarchs, and as it exists today, was primeval and universal is very deeply rooted. This is not surprising. To reverse the gaze of men from themselves is no easy task. The predominance of the male over the female, of the man over the woman and of the father over the mother, has been accepted, almost without question, in a civilisation built up on the recognition of male values and male standards of opinion. Thus the institutions, habits, prejudices, and superstitions of the patriarchal authority rest like an incubus upon us. The women of today carry the dead load upon their backs, and literally stagger beneath the accumulating burden of the ages.

The "Woman's Movement" is pressing us forward towards a recasting of the patriarchal view of the relative position and duties of the two sexes. It must be regarded as an extremely great and comprehensive movement affecting the whole of life. From this wider standpoint, the fight for the parliamentary suffrage is but as the vestibule to progress; the possession of the vote being no more than a necessary condition for attaining far larger and more fundamental ends.

It is, however, very necessary to remark that the recognition of this imposes a great responsibility upon women. For one thing, the practical difficulties of the present must be faced. It is far from easy to readjust existing conditions to meet the new demands. Present social and economic conditions are to a great extent chaotic. We cannot safely cast aside, in any haste for reform, those laws, customs and opinions which it has been the slow task of our civilisation to establish, not for men only, but for women. We women have to work out many questions far more thoroughly than hitherto we have done. We owe this to our movement and to the world of men. It will serve nothing to pull down, unless we are ready also to build up. Freedom can be granted only to the self-disciplined.

"Thou that does know the Self and the not-Self, expert in every work: endowed with self-restraint and perfect same-sightedness towards every creature free from the sense of I and my — thy power and energy are equal to my own, and thou hast practised the most severe discipline."[1]

This little book is an attempt to establish the position of the mother in the family. It sets out to investigate those early states of society, when, through the widespread prevalence of descent through the mother, the survival of the family clan and, in some cases, the property rights were dependent on women and not on men. I start from the belief that the mother was at one period the dominant partner in the sexual relationships. This does not, however, at all necessarily involve "rule by women." We must be very clear here. What I claim is this. The system by which the family was built up and grouped around the mother conferred special rights on women. The form of marriage favourable to this influence was that by which the husband entered the wife's family and clan, and lived there as a "consort-guest." The wife and mother was director in the home, the owner of the meagre property, the distributor of food, and the controller of the children.[2] Hence arises what is known as mother-right.

I am prompted to this inquiry by two reasons: in the first place, the origin of the maternal-system and the subsequent association of the mother and the father appear to me to afford evidence of the working of a natural law of the two sexes, which, both for social and other reasons, is of great interest in the present stage of women's history. The establishing of the mother's position is of great importance. If we can prove that women have exercised unquestioned and direct authority in the past history of human societies, we shall be in a position to answer those who today wish to set limits to women's activities. Then, in the second place, I am compelled to doubt certain conclusions, both of those who accept mother-right, and also of the greater number who now deny its occurrence. If I am right, and the importance of the maternal family has been unduly neglected and the true explanation of its origin overlooked, I feel that, whatever errors I may fall into, I am justified in undertaking this task. My mistakes will be corrected by others with more knowledge than I can claim; and if my theory of mother-right has any merit, it will be established in more competent hands. The vast majority of investigators on these questions are men. I am driven to believe that sometimes they are mistaken in their interpretation of habits and customs which arose among primitive societies in which the influence of women was marked. In dealing with the family and its origin it has been usual to consider the male side and to pass over the female members. This has led, I am sure, to much error.

The custom of tracing descent through the mother, either practised consciously and completely, or only as a survival, occurs among many primitive peoples in all parts of the world. Whether, however, it existed universally and from all time, or whether only in certain races, among whose institutions it remains or may still be traced, is a much debated question. Not all barbarous tribes are in the stage of mother-right; on the contrary many reckon descent through the father. But even where the latter is the case, vestiges of the former system are frequently to be found. There seems to be a common tendency to discredit a system of relationship, which suggests even as a bare possibility the mother, and not the father, being the head of the family. Yet, I believe I can assign some, at least plausible, reasons for believing that descent through women has been a stage, though not, I think, the first stage, in social growth for all branches of the human family.

There can be little doubt of the importance of kinship and inheritance being reckoned through the mother. If the children belong to her, and if by marriage the husband enters her home, the greater influence, based on the present possession of property, and the future hope of the family rests on the female side. Such conditions must have exercised strong influence on the position of the women members of the primitive clan and the honour in which they were held. It cannot be ignored.

Of course, this does not prevent the hardships of savage life weighing more heavily in many ways upon women than on the stronger men. In primitive societies, women have a position quite as full of anomalies as they hold among civilised races. Among some tribes, their position is extremely good; among others it is undoubtedly bad, but, speaking generally, it is much better than usually it is held to be.[3] Obviously, the causes must be sought in the environment and in social organisation. The differences in the status and power of women, often occurring in tribes at the same level of progress, would seem to be dependent largely on economic conditions. The subject is full of difficulties. Not only is the position of women thus variable, but our knowledge of the matter is very defective. It is seldom, indeed, that the question has been considered of sufficient importance to receive accurate attention.[4] Not infrequently conflicting accounts are given by different authorities, and even by the same writer.

I wish it to be understood that mother-right does not necessarily imply mother-rule. This system may even be combined with the patriarchal authority of the male. The unfortunate use of the term *Matriarchate* has led to much confusion. My own knowledge and study of primitive customs and ancient civilisations have made it plain to me that there has been a constant rise and fall of male and female dominance, but, I believe, that, on the whole, the superiority of women has been more frequent and more successful than that of men.

It is this that I shall attempt to prove.

The theory of mother-right has been subjected to so much criticism that a re-examination of the position is very necessary. To show its prevalence, to establish some leading points in its history, to make out its connection with the patriarchal family, and to trace the transition by which one system passed into the other, appear to me to be matters primarily important. The limited compass of this little book will prevent my substantiating my own views as I should wish, with a full and systematic survey of all authentic accounts of the peoples among whom mother-descent may be studied. I have considered, however, that I could summarise the position in a comprehensive picture, that will, I hope, suggest a point of view that seems to me to have been very generally neglected.

It is necessary to enter into such an inquiry with caution; the difficulties before me are very great. Nothing would be easier than from the mass of material available to pile up facts in furnishing a picture of the high status of women among many tribes under the favourable influence of mother-descent, that would unnerve any upholders of the patriarchal view of the subordination of women. It is just possible, on the other hand, to interpret these facts from a fixed point of thought of the father's authority as the one support of the family, and then to argue that, in spite of the mother's control over her children and over property, she still remained the inferior partner. I wish to do neither. It is my purpose to examine the evidence, and so to discover to what extent the system of tracing descent through the female side conferred any special claim for consideration upon women. I shall try to avoid mistakes. I put forward my own opinions with great diffidence. It is so easy, as I realise full well, to interpret facts by the bias of one's own wishes. I know that the habits and customs of primitive peoples that I have studied closely are probably few in comparison with those I have missed; yet to me they appear of such importance in the light they throw on the whole question of the relationships of the two sexes, that it seems well to bring them forward.

Since my attention, now many years ago, was first directed to this question, I have felt that a clear and concise account of the mother-age was indispensable for women. Such an account, with a criticism of the patriarchal theory, is here offered. Throughout I have attempted to clear up and bring into uniformity the two opposing theories of the origin of the human family. I have tried to gather the facts, very numerous and falling into several classes, by which the theory of the mother-age could be supported. And first it was necessary to clear out of the way a body of opinion, the prevalence of which has opposed an obstacle to the acceptance of the rights of mothers in the family relationship. The whole question turns upon which you start with; the man — the woman, or the woman — the man.

Here it should be explained that this little book is an expansion of the historical section which treats of "the Mother-Age Civilisation" in my former book, *The Truth about Woman.* I wish to take this opportunity of expressing my gratitude for the generous interest and sympathy with which my work has been received. Such kindness is very imperfectly repaid by an author's thanks; it is certainly the best incentive to further work.

This little volume was suggested to me by a review in one of the Suffrage papers. The writer, after speaking of the interest to women of the mother-age and the difficulty there was in gaining information on the subject, said that "a small and cheaper book on the matriarchate would be useful to women in all countries." I was grateful for this suggestion. I at once felt that I wanted to write such a book. For one thing, this particular section on the mother-age in *The Truth About Woman*, and my belief in the favourable influence of mother-descent on the status of women, has been much questioned. I have been told that I "had quite deliberately gone back to our uncivilised ancestors to 'fish up' the precedent of the matriarchate;" that I "had allowed my prejudices to dictate my choice of material, and had thus brought forward examples explanatory of my own opinions;" that I "had fastened eagerly on these, without inquiring too carefully about other facts having a contrary tendency." I was reminded of what I well knew, that the matriarchate and promiscuity with which it is usually connected were not universally accepted by anthropologists; the tendency today being to discredit both as being among the early phases of society. It was suggested that I "had unprofitably spent my time on the historical section of my book, and had built up my theory on a curiously uncertain foundation;" that I "had relied too much on the certain working of mother-right, and had been by no means clear in showing how, from such a position of power, women had sunk into subservience to patriarchal rule." In fact, it has seemed to be the opinion of my critics that I had allowed what I "would have liked to have happened to affect my account of what did happen in the infancy of man's social life."

Now, I want to say quite frankly, that I feel much of this criticism is just. The inquiry on the mother-age civilisation was only one small section of my book on Woman. I realise that very much was hurried over. There is on this subject of the origin of the family a literature so extensive, and such a variety of opinions, that the work of the student is far from easy. The whole question is too extensive to allow anything like adequate treatment within the space of a brief, and necessarily insufficient, summary. My earlier investigation may well be objected to as not being in certain points supported by sufficient proofs. I know this. It is not easy to condense the marriage customs and social habits of many different peoples into a few dozen pages. Of course, I selected my examples. But this I may say; I chose those which had brought me to accept mother-right. I was driven to this belief by my own study and reading long before the time of writing my book. What I really tried to do was to present to others the facts that had convinced me. But my stacks of unused notes, collected for my own pleasure during many years of work, are witness to how much I had to leave out.

I know that many objections that have been raised to the theory of mother-right were left unanswered. I dismissed much too lightly the patriarchal theory of the origin of the family, which during late years has gained such advocacy. I failed to carry my inquiry far enough back. I accepted with too little caution an early period of promiscuous sexual relationships. I did not make clear the stages in the advance of the family to the clan and the tribe; nor examine with sufficient care the later transition period in which mother-right gave place to father-right.

I have been sent back to examine again my own position. And to do this, it was necessary first to take up the question from the position of those whose views are in opposition to my own. I have made a much more extensive study of those authorities who, rejecting mother-right, accept a modification of the patriarchal theory as the origin of the family. This has led to some considerable recasting of my views. Not at all, however, to a change in my belief in mother-right, which, indeed, has now been strengthened, and, as I trust, built up on surer foundations.

By a fortunate chance, I was advised to read Mr Andrew Lang's *Social Origins*,[5] which work includes Mr Atkinson's *Primal Law*. I am greatly indebted to the assistance I have gained from these writers. It is, perhaps, curious that a very careful study of the patriarchal family as it is presented by Mr Atkinson and Mr Lang, has brought me to a conclusion fundamentally at variance from what might have been expected. I have gained invaluable support for my own belief in mother-right, and have found fresh proofs from the method of difference. I have cleared up many points that previously puzzled me. I am able now to accept the patriarchal theory, without at all shaking my faith in a subsequent period of mother-descent and mother-power.

The discussion on this question is now half a century old. Yet in spite of the opposition of many investigators, and the support of others, the main problems are still unsettled. What form did the family take in its earliest stage? Did it start as a small group or with the clan or horde? What were the earliest conditions of the sexual relationships? Was promiscuity at one period the rule? Was the foundation of the family based on the authority of the father, or of the mother? If on that of the father, how is mother-kin and mother-right to be explained? These are among the questions that must be answered. Not till this is done, can we establish any theory of mother-descent, or estimate its effect on the status of women.

The whole subject is a very wide and complicated one. If I differ on several important points from learned authorities, whose knowledge and research far exceed my own, I do so only after great hesitation, and because I must. The facts they have collected from their personal knowledge of primitive peoples (facts which I have gratefully used) often suggest quite opposite conclusions to my thoughts than to theirs — the viewpoint is different, that is all. They were seeking for one thing; I for another: they were men; I am a woman. It would be foolishness for me to attempt any special pleadings for my own opinions. How far I shall succeed, or fail, to make clear to others a period of mother-right that is certain to me, I do not know. I offer my little book with all humility, and yet without any apology. We may read and learn and gather knowledge from many sources; but the opinions of others we cannot take on credit; we must re-think them out for ourselves, and make them our own.

An Exposition of Bachofen's Theory of the Matriarchate

FIFTY-THREE YEARS ago in his great work, *Das Mutterrecht*,[6] the Swiss writer, Bachofen, drew the attention of the world to the fact that a system of kinship through mothers only prevailed among many primitive peoples, while survivals of the custom could be widely, if but faintly, traced among civilised races. Drawing his evidence from the actual statements of old writers, but more from legends and the mythologies of antiquity, he came to the conclusion that a system of descent through women had, in all cases, preceded the rise of kinship through males. Almost at the same time Dr J F McLennan,[7] ignorant of the work of Bachofen, came to the same opinion. This led to a reconsideration of the patriarchal theory; and for a time it was widely held that in the early stages of society a matriarchate prevailed, in which women held the supreme power. Further support came from Morgan, with his knowledge of the maternal family among American aborigines, and he was followed by Professor Tylor, McGee, and many other investigators.

Obviously this gynaecocratic view, which placed woman in a new relation to man, was unlikely to be permanently accepted. Thus a reaction to the earlier theory of the patriarchal family has set in, especially in recent years. Many writers, while acknowledging the existence of mother descent, deny that such a system carries with it, except in a few exceptional cases, mother-rights of special advantage to women; even when these seem to be present they believe such rights to be more apparent than real.

In bringing forward any theory of mother-right, it thus becomes necessary to show the causes that have led to this reversal in opinion. To do this, the first step will be to examine, with considerable detail, the evidence for the matriarchal theory as it is given by its two great supporters. Now, an interesting point arises, if we compare the view of Bachofen with that held by McLennan. No two ways could well be further apart than those by which these two men arrived at the same conclusion. Both accept an early period of promiscuous sexual relationships. But Bachofen found the explanation of mother-descent in the supremacy of women, and believed a matriarchate to have been established by them in a moral revolt against such *hetairism*. Mr McLennan, on the other hand, regarded the custom as due to uncertainty of paternity — the children were called after the mother because the father was unknown.

Let us concentrate our attention on the *Das Mutterrecht* of Bachofen, whose work as the great champion of matriarchy claims our most careful consideration. And it is necessary to say at once that there can be no doubt his view of women's supremacy is greatly exaggerated. Such a rule of women, at the very early stage of society when mother-kin is supposed to have arisen, is not proved, and does not seem probable. Even if it existed, *it could not have originated in the way and for the reasons* that are credited by the Swiss writer. I wish to emphasise this point. Much of the discredit that has fallen on the matriarchate has arisen, I am certain, through the impossibility of accepting Bachofen's mythical account of its origin. This great supporter of women was a dreamer, rather than a calm and impartial investigator. Founding his main theory on assumptions, he asks us to accept these as historical facts. Much of his work and his belief in women must be regarded as the rhapsodies of a poet. And yet, it is the poet who finds the truth. The poetic spirit is, in one sense, the most practical of all. Bachofen saw the fact of mother-power, though not *why* it was the fact, and he enfolded his arguments in a garment of pure fiction.

To disengage from his learned book, *Das Mutterrecht,*[8] his theory of the origin of the Matriarchate is no easy task. There is, for one thing, such bewildering contradiction and confusion in the material used. Then the interpretation of the mythical tales, so freely intermingled everywhere, is often strained — prompted by a poetic imagination which snatches at every kind of allegory. Often the views expressed are inconsistent with each other, the arguments and proofs are disconnected, while many of the details are hopelessly obscure and confused. Yet it seems to me possible to recognise the idea which brings into unity the mass of his work — the spirit, as it were, that breathes into it its life. It may be found in the clear appreciation of the superstitious and mystical element in primitive man, and their close interweaving with the sexual life. As I understand Herr Bachofen, the sex-act was the means which first opened up ways to great heights, but also to great depths.

Bachofen strongly insists on the religious element in all early human thought. He believes that the development of the primitive community only advanced by means of religious ideas. "Religion," he says, "is the only efficient lever of all civilisation. Each elevation and depression of human life has its origin in a movement which begins in this supreme department."[9]

The authority for this belief is sought in religious myths.

> Mythical tradition appears to be the faithful interpretation of the progress of the law of life, at a time when the foundations of the historical development of the ancient world were laid; it reveals the original mode of thought, and we may accept this direct revelation as true from our complete confidence in this source of history.[10]

This mystical religious element, which is the essential part of *Das Mutterrecht,* is closely connected by Bachofen with the power of women. As it is his belief that, even at this early period, the religious impulse was more developed among women than men, he bases on this unproved hypothesis his theory of women's supremacy. "Wherever gynaecocracy meets us," he says, "the mystery of religion is bound up with it, and lends to motherhood an incorporation in some divinity."[11]

Doubtless, this theory of a higher feminine spirituality is a pleasing one for women — but is it true? The insuperable difficulty to its acceptance arises, in the first place, from the fact that we can know nothing at all of the spiritual condition of the human beings among whom mother-kin was held first to have been practised. But we must go further than this in our doubt. Can we accept for any period a spiritual superiority in the character of woman over man? To me, at least, it is clear that a knowledge of the two sexes among all races both primitive and civilised — yes, and among ourselves, is sufficient to discredit such a supposition.

Bachofen would have us believe that[12] the mother-right of the ancient world, was due to a revolt of women against the degraded condition of promiscuity, which previously had been universal among mankind, a condition in which men had a community of wives, and *openly lived together like gregarious animals.*

"Women, by their nature nobler and more spiritual than men, became disgusted with this lawless *hetairism,* and, under the influence of a powerful religious impulse, combined in a revolt (the first Amazonian movement) to put an end to promiscuity and established marriage."

Over and over again Bachofen affirms this spiritual quality in women.

"The woman's religious attitude, in particular, the tendency of her mind towards the supernatural and the divine, influenced the man and robbed him of the position which nature disposed him to take in virtue of his physical superiority. In this way women's position was transformed by religious considerations, until they became in civil life what religion had caused them to be."[13] And again: "We cannot fail to see that of the two forms of gynaecocracy in question — religious and civil — the former was the basis of the latter. Ideas connected with worship came first, and the civil forms of life were then the result and expression."[14]

We may note in passing, the greater affectability of woman's nature, which would seem always to have had a tendency to expression in religio-erotic manifestations. But to build up a theory of matriarchy on this foundation is strangely wide of the facts. Bachofen adduces the spirituality of women as the cause of their power. But on what grounds can such a claim be supported?

It is on the evidence of licentious customs of all kinds and on polyandry, that he bases his belief in a period of promiscuity. He regards this early condition of *hetairism* as a law of nature, and believes that after its infraction by the introduction of individual marriage, expiation was required to be made to the Earth Goddess, Demeter, in temporary prostitution. Hence he explains the widespread custom of religious prostitution. This fanciful idea may be taken to represent Bachofen's method of interpretation. There is an intermediate stage between *hetairism* and marriage, such as the group-marriage, held by him to have been practised among barbarous peoples. "Each man has a wife, but they are all permitted to have intercourse with the wives of others."[15]

Great stress is laid on the acquisition by women of the benefits of a marriage law. In the families founded upon individual marriage, which grew up after the Amazonian revolt, the women, and not the men, held the first place. Bachofen does not tell us whether they assigned this place to themselves, or had it conceded to them. Women were the heads of the families, the children were named after the mother, and not the father, and all the relations to which rights of succession attached were traced through women only. All property was held by women. Moreover, from this headship, women assigned to themselves, or had conceded to them, the social and political power as well as the domestic supremacy.[16]

The authority for this remarkable theory is sought, with great ingenuity and patience, in the fragmentary accounts of barbarous people, and in an exhaustive study of heroic stories and religious myths. Bachofen argues powerfully for the acceptance of these myths.

> Every age unconsciously obeys, even in its poetry, the laws of its individual life. A patriarchal age could not, therefore, have invented the matriarchate, and the myths which describe the latter may be regarded as trustworthy witnesses of its historical existence. It may be taken for granted that the myths did not refer to special persons and occurrences, but only tell us of the social customs and ideas which prevailed, or were endeavouring to prevail, in several communities.[17]

This is true. It is the interpretation given to many of these myths that one is compelled to question. Bachofen's way of applying mythical tales has no scientific method; for one thing, abstract ideas are added to primitive legends which could only arise from the thought of civilised peoples. For instance, he accepts, without any doubt, the existence of the Amazons; and believes that the myths which refer to them record "a revolt for the elevation of the feminine sex, and through them of mankind." It is on such insecure foundations he builds up his matriarchal theory.

There is, however, an aspect of truth in Bachofen's position, which becomes plain on a closer examination. To prove this, I must quote a passage from *Das Mutterrecht,* as representing, or at least suggesting, the opinions of those who have argued most strongly against his theory. When recapitulating the facts and arguments in favour of accepting the supremacy of women, he makes this suggestive statement:

> The first state in all cases was that of *hetairism*. The rule is based upon the right of procreation: since there is no individual fatherhood, *all have only one father — the tyrant whose sons and daughters they all are, and to whom all the property belongs. From this condition in which the man rules by means*

> *of his rude sexual needs, we rise to that of gynaecocracy,* in which there is the dawn of marriage, of which the strict observance is at first observed by the woman, not by the man. Weary of always ministering to the lusts of man, *the woman raises herself by the recognition of her motherhood.* Just as a child is first disciplined by its mother, so are people by their women. It is only the wife who can control the man's essentially unbridled desires, and lead him into the paths of well-doing.... *While man went abroad on distant forays, the woman stayed at home, and was undisputed mistress of the household.* She took arms against her foe, and was gradually transformed into an Amazon.[18]

The italics in the passage are mine, for they bear directly on what I shall afterwards have to prove: (1) that mother-right was not the first stage in the history of the human family; (2) that its existence is not inconsistent with the patriarchal theory. Bachofen here suggests a pre-matriarchal period in which the elementary family-group was founded on and held together by a common subjection to the oldest and strongest male. This is the primordial patriarchal family.

Then come the questions: Can we accept mother-right? Are there any reasonable causes to explain the rise of female dominance? Westermarck, in criticising the matriarchal theory, has said: "The inference that 'kinship through females only' has everywhere preceded the rise of 'kinship through males,' would be warranted only on condition that the cause, or the causes, to which the maternal system is owing, could be proved to have operated universally in the past life of mankind."[19] Now, this is what I believe I am able to do. Hence it has been necessary first to clear the way of the old errors. Bachofen's interpretation is too fanciful to find acceptance. Will any one hold it as true that the change came because *women willed it*? Surely it is a pure dream of the imagination to credit women, at this supposed early stage of society, with rising up to establish marriage, in a revolt of purity against sexual licence, and moreover effecting the change by force of arms! Bachofen would seem to have been touched with the Puritan spirit. I am convinced also that he understood very little of the nature of woman. Conventional morality has always acted on the side of the man, not the woman. The clue is, indeed, given in the woman's closer connection with the home, and in the idea that "she raises herself by the recognition of her motherhood." But the facts are capable of an entirely different interpretation. It will be my aim to give a quite simple, and even commonplace, explanation of the rise of mother-descent and mother-right in place of the spiritual hypothesis of Bachofen.

It will be well, however, to examine further Bachofen's own theory. It is his opinion that the first Amazonian revolt and period of women's rule was followed by a second movement:

> Woman took arms against her foe [*i. e.* man], and was gradually transformed into an Amazon. *As a rival to the man the Amazon became hostile to him, and began to withdraw from marriage and from motherhood. This set limits to the rule of women, and provoked the punishment of heaven and men.*[20]

There is a splendid imaginative appeal in this remarkable passage. Again the italics are mine. It is, of course, impossible to accept this statement, as Bachofen does, as an historical account of what happened through the agency of women at the time of which he is treating. Yet, we can find a suggestion of truth that is eternal. Is there not here a kind of prophetic foretelling of every struggle towards readjustment in the relationships of the two sexes, through all the periods of civilisation, from the beginning until now? You will see what I mean. The essential fact for woman — and also for man — is the sense of community with the race. Neither sex can keep a position apart from parenthood. Just in so far as the mother and the father attain to consciousness and responsibility in their relations to the race do they reach development and power. Bachofen, as a poet, understood this; to me, at least, it is the something real that underlies all the delusion of his work. But I diverge a little in making these comments.

Again the origin of the change from the first period of matriarchy is sought by Bachofen in religion.

"Each stage of development was marked by its peculiar religious ideas, produced by the dissatisfaction with which the dominating idea of the previous stage was regarded; a dissatisfaction which led to a disappearance of this condition." "What was gained by religion, fostering the cause of women, by assigning a mystical and almost divine character to motherhood was now lost through the same cause. The loss came in the Greek era. Dionysus started the idea of the divinity of fatherhood; holding the father to be the child's true parent, and the mother merely the nurse." In this way, we are asked to believe, the rights of men arose, the father came to be the chief parent, the head of the mother and the owner of the children, and, therefore, the parent through whom kinship was traced. We learn that, at first, "women opposed this new gospel of fatherhood, and fresh Amazonian risings were the common feature of their opposition." But the resistance was fruitless. "Jason put an end to the rule of the Amazons in Lemnos. Dionysus and Bellerophon strove together passionately, yet without gaining a decisive victory, until Apollo, with calm superiority, finally became the conqueror, and the father gained the power that before had belonged to the mother."[21]

But before this took place, Bachofen relates yet another movement, which for a time restored the early matriarchate. The women, at first opposing, presently became converts to the Dionysusian gospel, and were afterwards its warmest supporters. Motherhood became degraded. Bacchanalian excesses followed, which led to a return to the ancient *hetairism*. Bachofen believes that this formed a fresh basis for a second gynaecocracy. He compares the Amazonian period of these later days with that in which marriage was first introduced, and finds that "the deep religious impulse being absent, it was destined to fail, and give place to the spiritual Apollonic conception of fatherhood."[22]

In Bachofen's opinion this triumph of fatherhood was the final salvation. This is what he says:

It was the assertion of fatherhood which delivered the mind from natural appearances, and when this was successfully achieved, human existence was raised above the laws of natural life. The principal of motherhood is common to all the spheres of animal life, but man goes beyond this tie in gaining pre-eminence in the process of procreation, and thus becomes conscious of his higher vocation. In the paternal and spiritual principle he breaks through the bonds of tellurism, and looks upwards to the higher regions of the cosmos. Victorious fatherhood thus becomes as distinctly connected with the heavenly light as prolific motherhood is with the teeming earth.[23]

Here, Bachofen, as is his custom, turns to point an analogy with the process of nature.

> All the stages of sexual life from Aphrodistic *hetairism* to the Apollonistic purity of fatherhood, have their corresponding type in the stages of natural life, from the wild vegetation of the morass, the prototype of conjugal motherhood, to the harmonic law of the Uranian world, to the heavenly light which, as the *flamma non urens*, corresponds to the eternal youth of fatherhood. The connection is so completely in accordance with law, that the form taken by the sexual relation in any period may be inferred from the predominance of one or other of these universal ideas in the worship of a people.[24]

Such, in outline, is Bachofen's famous matriarchal theory. The passages I have quoted, with the comments I have ventured to give, make plain the poetic exaggeration of his view, and sufficiently prove why his theory no longer gains any considerable support. To build up a dream-picture of mother-rule on such foundations was, of necessity, to let it perish in the dust of scepticism. But is the downthrow complete? I believe not. A new structure has to be built up on a new and surer foundation, and it may yet appear that the prophetic vision of the dreamer enabled Bachofen to see much that has escaped the sight of those who have criticised and rejected his assumption that power was once in the hands of women.

One great source of confusion has arisen through the acceptance by the supporters of the matriarchate of the view that men and women lived originally in a state of promiscuity. This is the opinion of Bachofen, of McLennan, of Morgan, and also of many other authorities, who have believed maternal descent to be dependent on the uncertainty of fatherhood. It will be remembered that Mr McLennan brought forward his theory almost simultaneously with that of Bachofen. The basis of his view is a belief in an ancient communism in women. He holds that the earliest form of human societies was the group or horde, and not the family. He affirms that these groups can have had no idea of kinship, and that the men would hold their women, like their other goods, in common, which is, of course, equal to a general promiscuity. There he agrees with Bachofen's belief in unbridled *hetairism*, but a very different explanation is given of the change which led to regulation, and the establishment of the maternal family.

According to Mr McLennan, the primitive group or horde, though originally without explicit consciousness of relationships, were yet held together by a *feeling* of kin. Such feeling would become conscious first between the mother and her children, and, in this way, mother-kin must have been realised at a very early period. Mr McLennan then shows the stages by which the savage would gradually, by reflection, reach a knowledge of the other relationships through the mother, sister and brother relationships, mother's brother and mother's sister, and all the degrees of mother-kin, at a time before the father's relation to his children had been established. The children, though belonging at first to the group, would remain attached to the mothers, and the blood-tie established between them would, as promiscuity gave place to more regulated sexual relationships, become developed into a system. All inheritance would pass through women only, and, in this way, mother-right would tend to be more or less strongly developed.

The mother would live alone with her children, the only permanent male members of the family being the sons, who would be subordinate to her. The husband would visit the wife, as is the custom under polyandry, which form of the sexual relationship Mr McLennan believes was developed from promiscuity — a first step towards individual marriage. Even after the next step was taken, and the husband came to live with his wife, his position was that of a visitor in her home, where she would have the protection of her own kindred. She would still be the owner of her children, who would bear her name, and not the father's; and the inheritance of all property would still be in the female line.[25]

We have here what appears to be a much more reasonable explanation of mother-kin and mother-right than that of Bachofen. Yet many have argued powerfully against it. Westermarck especially, has shown that belief in an early stage of promiscuous relationship is altogether untenable.[26] It is needless here to enter into proof of this.[27] What matters now is that with the giving up of promiscuity the whole structure of McLennan's theory falls to pieces. He takes it for granted that at one period paternity was unrecognised; but this is very far from being true. The idea of the father's relationship to the child is certainly known among the peoples who trace descent through the mother; the system is found frequently where strict monogamy is practised. Again, Mr McLennan connects polyandry with mother-descent, regarding the custom of plurality of husbands as a development from promiscuity. Here, too, he has been proved to be in error. Whatever the causes of the origin of polyandry, it has no direct connection with mother-kin, although it is sometimes practised by peoples who observe that system.

For myself, I incline to the opinion that the system by which inheritance passes through the mother needs no explanation. It was necessarily (and, as I believe, is still) the *natural* method of tracing descent. Moreover, it was adopted as a matter of course by primitive peoples among whom property considerations had not arisen. Afterwards what had started as a habit was retained as a system.

The reasons for naming children after the mother did not rest on relationship, the earliest question was not one of kinship, but of association. Those were counted as related to one another who dwelt together.[28] The children lived with the mother, and therefore, as a matter of course, were called after her, and not the father, who did not live in the same home.

All these questions will be understood better as we proceed with our inquiry. The important thing to fix in our minds is that mother-kin and mother-right (contrary to the opinion of McLennan and others) may very well have arisen quite independently of dubious fatherhood. It thus becomes evident that the maternal system offers no evidence for the hypothesis of promiscuity; we shall find, in point of fact, that it arose out of the regulation of the sexual relations, and had no connection with licence. It is necessary to understand this clearly.

Bachofen is much nearer to what is likely to have happened in the first stage of the family than Mr McLennan, though he also mistakenly connects the maternal system with unregulated *hetairism*. Still he suggests (though it would seem quite unconsciously) the patriarchal hypothesis, which founds the family first on the brute-force of the male. Mother-right has been discredited chiefly, as far as I have been able to find, because it is impossible to accept, at this early period, sexual conditions of the friendly ownership of women, entirely opposed to what was the probable nature of brute man. At this stage the eldest male in the family would be the ruler, and he would claim sexual rights over all the women in the group. Bachofen postulates a revolt of women to establish marriage. We have seen that such a supposition, in the form in which he puts it, is without any credible foundation. Yet, it is part of my theory that there was a revolt of women, or rather a combination of the mothers of the group, which led to a change in the direction of sexual regulation and order. But the causes of such revolt, and the way in which it was accomplished, were, in my opinion, entirely different from those which Bachofen supposes. The arguments in support of my view will be given in the next two chapters.

Difficulties and Objections : An Attempt to Reconcile Mother-Right with the Patriarchal Theory

THE FOUNDATION OF the patriarchal theory is the jealous sexual nature of the male. This is important; indeed profoundly significant. The strongest argument against promiscuity is to be gained from what we know of this factor of jealousy in the sexual relationships.

"The season of love is the season of battle," says Darwin. Such was the law passed on to man from millions of his ancestral lovers. The action of this law[29] may be observed at its fiercest intensity among man's pre-human ancestors. Courtship without combat is rare among all male quadrupeds, and special offensive and defensive weapons for use in these love-fights are found; for this is the sex-tragedy of the natural world, the love-tale red-written in blood.

This factor of sexual jealousy — the conflict of the male for possession of the female — has not been held in sufficient account by those who regard promiscuity as being the earliest stage in the sexual relationships. That jealousy is still a powerful agent even in the most civilised races is a fact on which it is unnecessary to dwell. This being so, and since the action of jealousy is so strong in the animal kingdom, it cannot be supposed to have been dormant among primitive men. Rather, in the infancy of his history this passion must have acted with very great intensity. Thus it becomes impossible to accept any theory of the community of women in the earliest stage of the family. For inevitably such peaceful association would be broken up by jealous battles among the males, in which the strongest member would kill or drive away his rivals.

Great stress is laid by the supporters of promiscuity on the danger that such conflicts must have been to the growing community. It is, therefore, held that in order to prevent this check on their development, it was necessary for the male members not to give way to jealousy, but to be content with promiscuous ownership of women. But this is surely to credit savage man with a control of the driving jealous instinct that he could not then have had? What we do not find in the sexual conduct of men, as they now are, cannot be credited as existing in the infancy of social life. We fall into many mistakes in judging these questions of sex; we under-estimate the strength of love-passion — the uncounted ancestral forces dating back to the remote beginnings of life. Doubtless conflicts over the possession of women were frequent from the beginning of man's history. But these disputes would not lead to promiscuous intercourse, only to a change in the tyrant male, who ruled over the women in the group.

Another fact against a belief in promiscuity is that the lowest savages known to us are not promiscuous, in so far as there is no proved case of the sexual relations being absolutely unregulated. They all recognise sets of women with whom certain sets of men can have no marital relations. Again these savages are very far removed from the state of man's first emergence from the brute, as is proved by their combination into large and friendly tribes. Such peaceful aggregation could only have arisen at a much later period, and after the males had learnt by some means to control their brute appetites and jealousy of rivals in that movement towards companionship, which, first resting in the sexual needs, broadens out into the social instincts.

For these reasons, then, we conclude that the theory of a friendly union having existed among males in the primitive group is the very reverse of the truth. This question has now been sufficiently proved. I am thus brought into agreement with Dr Westermarck, Mr Crawley, and Mr Lang, in his examination of Mr Atkinson's *Primal Law*, as well as with other writers, all of whom have shown that promiscuity cannot be accepted as a stage in the early life of the human family.

I have now to show how far this rejection of promiscuity affects our position with regard to mother-descent and mother-right. It is clearly of vital importance to any theory that its foundations are secure. One foundation — that of promiscuity, on which Bachofen and McLennan, the two upholders of matriarchy, base their hypothesis — has been overthrown. It thus becomes necessary to approach the question from an altogether different position. Mother-right must be explained without any reference to unregulated sexual conduct. I am thus turned back to examine the opposing theory to matriarchy, which founds the family on the patriarchal authority of the father. Nor is this all. What we must expect a true theory to do is to show conditions that are applicable not only to special cases, but in their main features to mankind in general. I have to prove that such conditions arose in the primitive patriarchal family as it advanced towards social aggregation, that would not only make possible, but, as I believe, would necessitate the power of the mothers asserting its force in the group-family. Only when this is done can I hope that a new belief in mother-right may find acceptance.

The patriarchal theory stated in its simplest form is this: Primeval man lived in small family groups, composed of an adult male, and of his wife, or, if he were powerful, several wives, whom he jealously guarded from the sexual advances of all other males. In such a group the father is the chief or patriarch as long as he lives, and the family is held together by their common subjection to him. As for the children, the daughters as soon as they grow up are added to his wives, while the sons are driven out from the home at the time they reach an age to be dangerous as sexual rivals to their father. The important thing to note is that *in each group there would be only one adult polygamous male, with many women of different ages and young children*. I shall return to this later. Such is the marked difference in the position of the two sexes — the solitary jealously unsocial father and the united mothers. I can but wonder how its significance has escaped the attention of the many inquirers, who have sought the truth in this matter. Probably the explanation is to be found in this: they have been interested mainly in one side of the family — the male side; I am interested in the other side — in the women members of the group. The position of women has seemed of primary importance to very few. Bachofen is almost alone in placing this question first, and his mystical far-fetched hypothesis has failed to find acceptance.

Let me now, in order to make the position clearer, continue a rough grouping of the supposed conditions in this primordial family, with all its members in subjection to the common father. It may be argued that we can know nothing at all about the family and the position of the two sexes at this brute period. This is true. The conditions are, of course, conjectural, and any suggested conclusions to be drawn from them must be still more so. Yet some hypothesis must be risked as a starting-point for any theory that attempts to go so far back in the stream of time.

We may suppose, then, that mankind aboriginally lived in small families in much the same way as the great monkeys: we see the same conditions, for instance, among the families of gorillas, where the group never becomes large. The male leader will not endure the rivalry of the young males, and as soon as they grow up a contest takes place, and the strongest and eldest male, by killing or driving out the others, maintains his position as the tyrant head of the family.[30]

This may be taken as a picture of the human brute-family. It is clear that the relation of the father to the other group members was not one of kinship, but of power. "Every female in my crowd is my property," says — or feels — Mr Atkinson's patriarchal anthropoid, "and the patriarch gives expression to his sentiment with teeth and claws, if he has not yet learned to double up his fist with a stone in it. These were early days."[31]

We may conclude that there would be many of these groups,

each with a male head, his wives and adult daughters, and children of both sexes. It is probable that they lived a nomadic life, finding a temporary home in a cave, rock, or tree-shelter, in some place where the supply of food was plentiful. The area of their wanderings would be fixed by the existence of other groups; for such groups would almost certainly be mutually hostile to each other, watchfully resenting any intrusion on their own feeding ground. A further, and more powerful, cause of hostility would arise from the sexual antagonism of the males. Around each group would be the band of exiled sons, haunting their former hearth-homes, and forming a constant element of danger to the solitary paternal tyrant. This I take to be important as we shall presently see. For, the most urgent necessity of these young men, after the need for food, must have been to obtain wives. This could be done only by capturing women from one or other of the groups. The difficulties attending such captures must have been great. It is, therefore, probable the young men at first kept together, sharing their wives in polyandrous union. But this condition would not continue, the group thus formed would inevitably break up at the adult stage under the influence of jealousy; the captured wives would be fought for and carried off by the strongest males to form fresh groups.

In this matter, I have given the opinion of Mr Atkinson and Mr Lang. They hold that no permanent peaceful union could have been maintained among the groups of young men and their captive wives. Mr Atkinson gives the reason:

> Their unity could only endure as long as the youthfulness of the members necessitated union for protection, and their immaturity prevented the full play of sexual passion.
>
> And again:
>
> The necessary Primal Law which alone could determine peace within a family circle by recognising a *distinction between female and male* (the indispensable antecedent to a definition of marital rights) could never have arisen in such a body. It

follows if such a law was ever evoked, it must have been from *within the only other assembly in existence*, viz. that headed by the solitary polygamous patriarch.[32]

Whether Mr Atkinson is right I shall not attempt to say; the point is one on which I hesitate a decided opinion; but as this view affords support to my own theory I shall accept it.

Now, to consider the bearing of this on our present inquiry. So far I have followed very closely the family group gathered around the patriarchal tyrant, under the conditions given by Mr Atkinson and Mr Lang, in *Social Origins and Primal Law*. It will not, I think, have escaped the notice of the reader that very little has been said about the women and their children. There is no hint at all that the women must have lived a life of their own, different in its conditions from that of the men. The female members, it would seem, have been taken for granted and not considered, except in so far as their presence is necessary to excite the jealous sexual combats of the males. This seems to be very instructive. The idea of the subjection of all females to the solitary male has been accepted without question. But the group consisted of *many women and only one adult man*. Yet in spite of this, the man is held to be the essential member; all the family obey him. His wife (or wives) and his daughters, though necessary to his pleasure as also to continue the group, are regarded as otherwise unimportant, in fact, mere property possessions to him. Now, I am very sure the rights these group-women must have held have been greatly underrated, and the neglect to recognise this has led, I think, to many mistakes. I am willing to accept the authority of the polygamous patriarch — within limits. But it seems probable, as I shall shortly indicate, that a predominant influence in the domestic life is to be ascribed to the women, and, therefore, "the movement towards peace within the group circle" must be looked for as a result from the feminine side of the family, rather than from the male side. There is still another point: I maintain that precisely through the concentration of the male ruler on the sexual subjection of his females, conditions must have arisen, affecting the conduct and character of the women: conditions, moreover, that would bring them inevitably more and more into a position of power.

It remains for me to suggest what I believe these conditions to have been. Meanwhile let us keep one fact steadily before our minds. The fierce sexual jealousy of the males had by some means to be controlled. It is evident that the way towards social progress could be found only by the peaceful aggregation of these solitary hostile groups; and this could not be done without breaking down the rule that strength and seniority in the male conferred upon him marital right over all the females. In other words, the tyrant patriarch had in some way to learn to tolerate the presence of other adult males on friendly terms within his own group. We have to find how this first, but momentous, step in social progress was taken.

Let us concentrate now our attention on the domestic life of the women. And first we must examine more carefully the exact conditions that we may suppose to have existed in these hostile groups. The father is the tyrant of the band — an egoist. Any protection he affords the family is in his own interests, he is chief much more than father. His sons he drives away as soon as they are old enough to give him any trouble; his daughters he adds to his harem. We may conceive that the domination of his sexual jealousy must have chiefly occupied his time and his attention. It is probable that he was fed by his women; at least it seems certain that he cannot have provided food for them and for all the children of the group. Sex must have been uninterruptedly interesting to him. In the first place he had to capture his wife, or wives, then he had to fight for the right of sole possession. Afterwards he had to guard his women, especially his daughters, from being carried off, in their turn, by younger males, his deadly rivals, who, exiled by sexual jealousy from his own and the other similar hearth-homes, would come, with each returning year, more and more to be feared. An ever-recurring and growing terror would dog each step of the solitary paternal despot, and necessitate an unceasing watchfulness against danger, and even an anticipation of death. For when old age, or sickness decreased his power of holding his own, then the tables would be turned, and the younger men, so hardly oppressed, would raise their hands against him in parricidal strife.

You will see what all this strife suggests — the unstable and adventitious relation of the man to the social hearth-group. Such conditions of antagonism of each male against every other male must favour the assumption that no advance in peace — on which alone all future progress depended — could have come from the patriarchs. Jealousy forced them into unsocial conduct.

But advance by peace to progress was by some means to be made. I believe that the way was opened up by women.

I hasten to add, however, in case I am mistaken here, that I am very far from wishing to set up any claim of superiority for savage woman over savage man. The momentous change was not, indeed, the result of any higher spiritual quality in the female, nor was it a religious movement, as is the beautiful dream of Bachofen. I do not think we can credit "a movement" as having taken place at all, rather the change arose gradually, inevitably, and quite simply. To postulate a conscious movement towards progress organised by women is surely absurd. Human nature does not start on any new line of conduct voluntarily, rather it is forced into it in connection with the conditions of life. Just as savage man was driven into unsocial conduct, so, as I shall try to show, savage woman was led by the same conditions acting in an opposite direction, into social conduct.

My own thought was drawn first to this conclusion by noting the behaviour of a band of female turkeys with their young. It was a year ago. I was staying in a Sussex village, and near by my home was the meadow of a farm in which families of young turkeys were being reared. Here I often sat; and one day it chanced that I was reading *Social Origins and Primal Law*. I had reached the chapter on "Man in the Brutal Stage," in which Mr Atkinson gives the supposed facts of brute man, and the action of his jealousy in the family group. I was very much impressed; my reason told me that what the author stated so well was probably right. Such sexually jealous conduct on the part of savage man was likely to be true; it was much easier to accept this than the state of promiscuous intercourse, with its friendly communism in women, in which I had hitherto believed. I really was very much disturbed. For I was still unshaken in my belief in mother-right. How were the two theories to be reconciled?

Often it is a small thing that points to the way for which one is seeking. All at once my little boy, who had been playing in the field, called out, "Oh, look at the Gobble-gobble," — the name by which he called the male-turkey. The cock, his great tail spread, his throat swelling, was swaggering across the field, making an immense amount of noisy disturbance. A group of females and young birds, many of them almost full grown, were near to where we were sitting; they had been rooting about in the ground getting their food. Their fear at the approach of the strutting male was manifest. All the band gathered together, with the young in the centre, led and flanked by the mothers. As the male continued to advance upon them, they retreated further and further, and finally took harbour in a barn. Here the swaggerer tried to follow them, but the rear females turned and faced him and drove him off.

I had found the clue that I was seeking. All I had been reading now had a clear meaning for me. In my delight, I laughed aloud. I saw the egoism of the solitary male; I knew the meaning of the females' retreat; they were guarding the young from the feared attacks of the father. I realised how the male's unsocial conduct towards his offspring had forced the females to unite with one another. The cock's strength, the gorgeous display of sex-charms, were powerless before this peaceful combination. He was alone, a tyrant — the destroyer of the family. But I saw, too, that his polygamous jealousy served as a means to the end of advance in progress. It was the male's non-social conduct that had forced social conduct upon the females. And I understood that the patriarchal tyrant was just the one thing I had been looking for. My belief in mother-power had gained a new and, as I felt then in the first delight of that discovery, and as I still feel, a much surer, because a simpler and more natural foundation.

Having now defined my position, and having related how such conviction came to me, let me proceed to examine the causes that would lead to the assertion of women's power, in the aboriginal family group. From what has been said, the following conditions acting on the women, may, it is submitted, be fairly deduced:

1) In the group, which comprised the mothers, the adult daughters, and the young of both sexes, the women would live on terms of association as friendly hearth-mates.

2) The strongest factor in this association would arise from the dependence of the children upon their mothers; a dependence that was of much longer duration than among the animals, on account of the pre-eminent helplessness of the human child, which entailed a more prolonged infancy.

3) The women and their children would form the group, to which the father was attached by his sexual needs, but remained always a member apart — a kind of jealous fighting specialisation.

4) The temporary hearth-home would be the shelter of the women; and it was under this shelter that children were born and the group accumulated its members. Whether cave, or hollow tree, or some frail shelter, the home must have belonged to the women.

5) And this state would necessarily attach the mothers to the home, much more closely than the father, whose desire lay in the opposite direction of disrupting the home. Moreover this attachment always would be present and acting on the female children, who, unless captured, would remain with the mothers, while it could never arise in the case of the sons, whose fate was to be driven from the home. Such conditions must, as time went on, have profoundly modified the women's outlook, bending their desires to a steady, settled life, conditions under which alone the germ of social organisation could develop.

6) Again, the daily search for the daily food must have been undertaken chiefly by the women. For it is impossible that one man,

however skilful a hunter, could have fed all the female members and children of the group. We may conceive that his attention and his time must have been occupied largely in fighting his rivals; while much of his strength, as sole progenitor, must have been expended in sex. It is therefore probable that frequently the patriarch was dependent on the food activities of his women.

7) The mothers, their inventive faculties quickened by the stress of childbearing and childrearing, would learn to convert to their own uses the most available portion of their environment. It would be under the attention of the women that plants were first utilised for food. Seeds would be beaten out, roots and tubers dug for, and nuts and fruits gathered in their season and stored for use. Birds would have to be snared, shellfish and fish would be caught; while, at a later period, animals would be tamed for service. Primitive domestic vessels to hold and to carry water, baskets to store the food supplies would have to be made. Clothes for protection against the cold would come to be fashioned. All the faculties of the women, in exercises that would lead to the development of every part of their bodies, would be called into play by the work of satisfying the physical needs of the group.

8) This interest and providence for the family would certainly have its effect on the development of the women. The formation of character is largely a matter of attention, and the attention of the mothers being fixed on the supply of the necessary food, doubtless often difficult to obtain, their energies would be driven into productive activities, much more than in the case of the father, whose attention was fixed upon himself.

9) In all these numerous activities the women of each group would work together. And through this co-operation must have resulted the assertion of the women's power, as the directors and organisers of industrial occupations. As the group slowly advanced in progress, such power increasing would raise the women's position; the mothers would establish themselves permanently as of essential value in the family, not only as the givers of life, but as the

chief providers of the food essential to the preservation of the life of its members.

10) And a further result would follow in the treatment by the male of this new order. The women by obtaining and preparing food would gain an economic value. Wives would become to the patriarch a source of riches, indispensable to him, not only on account of his sex needs, but on account of the more persistent need of food. Thus the more women he possessed the greater would be his own comfort, and the physical prosperity of the group. The women would become of ever greater importance, and the economic power that they thus acquired would more and more favourably influence their position.

11) There is one other matter in this connection. The greater number of women in the group the stronger would become their power of combination. I attach great importance to this. Working together for the welfare of all, the social motive would grow stronger in women, so that necessarily they would come to consider the collective interests of the group. Can it be credited that such conditions could have acted upon the patriarch, whose conduct would still be inspired by individual appetite and selfish inclinations? I maintain such a view to be impossible.

12) Another advantage, I think, would arise for women out of the male's jealous tyranny in the sexual relationship. Such an idea may appear strange, if we think only of the subjection of the females to the brute appetite of the patriarch. Yet there is another side. The women must have gained freedom by being less occupied with sex passions, and also from being less jealously interested in the man than he was in them. It may be urged that the women would be jealous of each other. I do not think this could have been. Jealousy has its roots in the consciousness of possession, and is only aroused through fear of loss. This could not have acted with any great power among the women in the patriarchal group. Their interest of possession in sex must have been less acute in consciousness than the interest of the male. Doubtless, the woman would be attracted by the male's courageous action in fighting his rivals for possession of

her, but when the rival was the woman's son such attraction would come into strong conflict with the deeper maternal instinct.

13) From the standpoint of physical strength, the patriarch was the master, the tyrant ruler of the group, who, doubtless, often was brutal enough. But the women, leading an independent life to some extent, and with their mental ingenuity developed by the conditions of their life, would learn, I believe, to outwit their master by passive united resistance. They would come to utilise their sex charms as an accessory of success. Thus the unceasing sexual preoccupation of the male, with the emotional dependence it entailed on the females, must, I would suggest, have given women an immense advantage. If I am right here, the patriarch would be in the power of his women, much more surely than they would be in his power.

14) Again, an antagonism must have arisen between the despot father and his women, in particular with his daughters, forced to submit to his brute-passions. I confess I find grave difficulty in reconciling the view that the group-daughters would willingly become the wives of their father. I cannot conceive them without some power to exercise that choice in love, which is the right of the female throughout nature. There is great insistence by Mr Atkinson, and all who have written on the subject, on the sexual passions of the males, while the desires of the women are not considered at all. Apparently they are held to have had none! This affords yet another instance of the strange concentration on the male side of the family. It is taken for granted, for instance, that in every case the young men, when driven from their home, had to capture their wives from other groups. I would suggest that often the capture was aided by the woman herself; she may even have escaped from the hearth-home in her desire to find a partner, preferring the rule of a young tyrant to an old one, who moreover was her father. I believe, too, that the wives and mothers must frequently have asserted their will in rebellion. I picture, indeed, these savage women ever striving for more privileges, and step by step advancing through peaceful combination to power.

15) I desire also to maintain that all I have here suggested finds

support from what is known of the position of women among primitive peoples; and I may add also, from the character of women today.

Now I have summarised briefly what seem to me the probable conditions of the women's daily life in these earliest groups. I have attempted to show how the sexual jealousy, which acted for the destruction of the mutually hostile male members, would necessitate for the women conditions in many ways favourable; conditions of union in which lay the beginnings of peace and order. What we have to fix in our thoughts is the significant fact of the sociability of the women's lives in contrast with the solitude of the jealous sire, watchfully resenting the intrusion of all other males. Such conditions cannot have failed to domesticate the women, and urged them forward to the work that was still to be done in domesticating man. During the development of the family, we may expect that the patriarch will seek to hold his rights, and that the women will exert their influence more and more in breaking these down; and this is precisely what we do find, as I presently shall show.

One point further. It may, of course, be urged that all I am affirming for women in this far back beginning is but a process of ingenious guessing. Such criticism is just. But I am speaking of conditions at a time when conjecture is necessary. I venture to say that my suggestions are in accord with what is likely to have happened. Moreover, many difficulties will be made clearer if these guesses are accepted. I believe that here in the earliest patriarchal stage we have already the germs of the maternal family. All the chances for success in power rested with the united mothers, rather than with the solitary father. Assuredly the jealous patriarchs paid a heavy price for their sexual domination.

Development in the Patriarchal Family and the Rise of Mother-Power

THE ESSENTIAL QUESTION, now, is how these small hostile groups were brought by association to expand into larger groups. In what way was the sexual monopoly of the male ruler first curbed, and afterwards broken down, for only by this being done could peace be gained? However advantageous the habits of the patriarch may have been for himself, they were directly opposed to progress. Jealousy depends on the failure to recognise the rights of others. This sexual egoism, by which one man through his strength and seniority held marital rights over all the females of his group, had to be struck at its roots. In other words, the solitary despot had to learn to tolerate the association of other adult males.

How was this happy change to be brought about? Social qualities are surely developed in the character by union with one's fellow beings. From what has been stated, it seems certain that it was in the interests of the women to consolidate the family, and by means of association to establish their own power. Jealousy is an absolutely non-social quality. Regarding its influence, it is certainly absurd to believe any voluntary association to have been possible among the males of the hostile patriarchal groups; to credit this is to give the lie to the entire theory. We are driven, therefore, to seek for the beginnings of social conduct among the women. I have suggested the conditions forcing them into combination with one another against the tyranny of the patriarch. I have now to show how these causes, continually acting, brought the women step by step into a position of authority and power. There is, however, no suggestion of a spiritual revolt on the part of women. I do not wish to set up any claim for, because I do not believe in, the superiority of one sex over the other sex. Character is determined by the conditions of living. If, as I conceive, progress came through savage women, rather than through savage men, it was because the conditions were really more favourable to them, and drove them on in the right path. However strange it may appear, their sexual subjection to the fierce jealousy of the patriarch acted as a means to an end in advancing peace.

The strongest force of union between the women would grow out of the consciousness of an ever-threatening and common danger. Not only had the young to be fed and cared for during infancy and childhood, but, as they grew in years, they had to be guarded from the father, whose relation to his offspring was that of an enemy. It has been seen how the sons were banished at puberty from the family group to maintain the patriarch's marital rights. Doubtless, the strength of maternal love gained in intensity through the many failures in conflicts, that must have taken place with the tyrant fathers. Would not this community of suffering tend to force the women to unite with one another, at each renewed banishment of their sons? May they not, after the banishment, have assisted their sons in the capture of their wives? I think it must be allowed that this is possible. And there is another point to notice. The exiled sons and their captured wives would each have a mother in the groups they had left. May it not be conceived that, as time brought progress in intelligence, some friendly communication might have been established between group and group, in defiance of the jealous guardianship of the patriarchs? Thus, through the danger, ever to be feared in every family, there might open up a way by sympathy to a possible future union.

It is part of my supposition that every movement towards

friendship must have arisen among the women. This is no fanciful idea of my own. Mr Atkinson, one of the strongest supporters of the patriarchal theory, agrees with this view, though he does not seem to see its origin, and does not follow up its deep suggestion. By him the movement in advance is narrowed to a single issue of peace between the father and his sons, but this great step is credited to the influence of the mothers. I must quote the passages that refer to this:[33]

> At the renewed banishment of each of her male progeny by the jealous patriarch, the mother's feelings and instincts would be increasingly lacerated and outraged. Her agonised efforts to retain at least her last and youngest would be even stronger than with her first born. It is exceedingly important to observe that her chances of success in this case would be much greater. When this last and dearest son approached adolescence, it is not difficult to perceive that the patriarch must have reached an age when the fire of desire may have become somewhat dull, whilst, again, his harem, from the presence of numerous adult daughters, would be increased to an extent that might have overtaxed his once more active powers. Given some such rather exceptional situation, where a happy opportunity in superlative mother love wrestled with a for once satiated paternal appetite in desire, we may here discern a possible key of the sociological problem which occupies us, and which consisted in a conjunction within one group of two adult males.

In the next paragraph the author presents the situation which in this way might have arisen:

> We must conceive that, in the march of the centuries, on some fateful day, the bloody tragedy in the last act of the familiar drama was avoided, and the edict of exile or death left unpronounced. *Pure maternal love triumphed over the demons of lust and jealousy.* A mother succeeded in keeping by her side a male child, and thus, by a strange coincidence, that father and son, who, amongst all mammals, had been the most deadly

enemies, were now the first to join hands. So portentous an alliance might well bring the world to their feet. The family would now present for the first time, the until then unknown spectacle of the inclusion within a domestic circle, and amidst its component females, of an adolescent male youth. It must, however, be admitted that such an event, at such an epoch, demanded imperatively very exceptional qualities, both physiological and psychological, in the primitive agents. The new happy ending to that old-world drama which had run so long through blood and tears, was an innovation requiring very unusually gifted actors. How many failures had doubtless taken place in its rehearsal during the centuries, with less able or happy interpreters!

Mr Atkinson supposes that success in the new experiment "was rendered possible by the rise of new powers in nascent man." Here I do not follow him. "The germ of altruism," which he sees as "already having risen to make its force felt" was, indeed, as he says "an important factor." But is it credible that this altruism existed in the father? I can conceive him being won over through his own emotional dependence on some specially pleasing woman; he may well have had favourites among his wives. I cannot accept "altruism" as a reason for his conduct, under conditions acting in an exact opposite way in fostering and increasing egoism. Much more probable is the supposition that he "must have reached the age when the fire of desire had become somewhat dulled."

I must also take exception to a further statement of Mr Atkinson, "that with such prolonged infancy there had been opportunity for the development of paternal philoprogenitiveness." And again: "It is evident that such long-continued presence of sons could but result in a certain mutual sympathy, however inevitable the eventual exile." It is unnecessary for me to labour this question. I may, however, point out, that the identical conditions of the family among the anthropoid apes (on whom Mr Atkinson bases his patriarchy) do not afford any proof of paternal altruism. The polygamous jealous father never enters into friendly union with the other males. He is strong and sexually beautiful, but he is never social in his domestic conduct. He is the tyrant in the family, and the young are guarded from his attacks by the mothers. With the mothers there is protection and safety, with the father ownership. The whole argument of the patriarchal theory is based on the fact of the jealous conduct of the male. Driven to live in solitary enmity, the patriarch could not voluntarily tolerate the presence of a rival, if he was to maintain his position as ruler. It is impossible to get away from this. Mr Atkinson comes very near to this essential truth, when he suggests (though he does not fully acknowledge) that the first step in social development came through the mother's love for her child; but at once he turns aside from this, drawn, I think unconsciously, to the common opinion of the complete subjection of the females to the male, an opinion always making it difficult to accept the initiative in reform as coming from the woman.

The exclusive and persisting idea of Mr Atkinson's theory is to establish the action of what he calls "the primal law." Only by limiting and defining the marital rights of the males over the females could advancement be gained. Until this was done these small hostile groups could not become larger, and expand into the clan or tribe.

I must follow this question a little although it leads us aside from the immediate subject of my own inquiry. The first step in progress has been taken; by the triumph of maternal love, an adult male son is now included in the group. We must conceive that this victory, having once been gained by one mother, would be repeated by other mothers. Afterwards, as time went on, the advantage in strength gained to the group by this increase in their male members, would tend to encourage the custom. One may reasonably assume that it became established as a habit in each group that once had taken the first step. Father and sons, for so long enemies, now enter on a truce.

It must not, however, be concluded that sexual peace followed this new order. It is part of Mr Atkinson's theory that the patriarch's sexual jealousy would not be broken down by his tolerance of the presence of his sons. Peace could be maintained only so long as the intruders respected his marital rights. Under this condition, all the group women, as they all belonged to the patriarch, would be taboo to the young men; otherwise there would be a fight, and the offending son would be driven into exile. Doubtless this frequently happened, but the advantages gained by union would tend to prevent the danger. Some means of preserving sexual peace within the group certainly would come to be established. "For the first time," as Mr Atkinson points out, "we encounter the factor which is to be the leading power in future metamorphosis, i. e. *an explicit distinction between female and female as such.*"

Through this bar placed on the female members within the family circle, the sons, who remained in peace, would be forced to continue the practice of capturing their wives, and would bring in women to live with them from other groups. It is assumed that these captures were in all cases hostile. I have given my reasons for disagreeing with this view. I hold that the young women may have been glad to have been taken by the young men, and most probably assisted them, in a surely not unnatural desire to escape from their tyrant fathers. I really cannot credit such continued sexual subjection on the part of the group-daughters, an opinion which arises, I am certain, from the curious misconception of the passivity of the human female in love.

I do not wish to conceal that my conjecture of an active part having been taken by the women, both in their captures and also in all the relationships of the family, is opposed to the great majority of learned opinion. The reason for this already has been suggested. Almost invariably the writers on these questions are men, and there is, I imagine, a certain blindness in their view. I am convinced that from the earliest beginnings of the human family women have exercised a much stronger and more direct influence than is usually believed. All the movements towards regulation and progress, so ingeniously worked out by Mr Atkinson, are easier to credit if we accept the initiative as having come from the group-mothers. I have an inward conviction of an unchanging law between the two sexes, and though I cannot here attempt to give any proof, it seems to me, we can always trace *the absorption by the male of female ideas.* The man accepts what the woman brings forward, and then assumes the control, believing he is the originator of her ideas. Take this case of capture: If, as I suggest, the young women assisted or even took the initiative in their own captures, they would very plainly not be willing to allow sexual relationships with another hoary patriarch. I would urge that here again it was by the action of the young women, rather than the young men, that the new order was established. But this is a small matter. If I am right, the communal living and common danger among the women would powerfully bind them together in union, and sever them from the male rulers. Once this is granted, it follows that social consciousness in the women must have been stronger than in the solitary males. Then there can be no possible doubt of the part taken by women in the slow advancement of the group by regulation to social peace. Moreover, I believe, that confirmation of what is here claimed for women will be found (as will appear in the later part of my inquiry) in many social habits among existing primitive peoples, who still live under the favourable conditions of the maternal family; habits that suggest a long evolutionary process, and that can be explained only if they have arisen in a very remote beginning. But enough on this subject has now been said.

Many interesting questions arise from the action of Mr Atkinson's "primal law." His theory offers a solution of the much-debated question of the origin of exogamy,[34] the term used first by Mr McLennan, in *Primitive Marriage,* for the rule which prohibited sexual relationships within the group limit. Continence imposed by the patriarch on his sons within the group, as a condition of his tolerance of their presence, necessarily and logically entailed marriage without, with women from some other group. This explanation of exogamy is so simple that it seems likely to be true. It is much more reasonable than any of the numerous other theories that have been brought forward. Mr McLennan, for instance, suggests that the custom arose through a scarcity of females, owing to the widespread practice of female infanticide. This can hardly be accepted, for such conditions, where they exist, would arise at a much later period. Even less likely is the theory of Dr Westermarck, who explains exogamy as arising from "an instinct against marriage of near kin." But we have no proof of the existence of any such instinct.[35] Mr Crawley's view is similar: he connects the custom with the idea of sexual taboo, which makes certain marriages a deadly sin. It is evident that these causes could not have operated with the brute patriarch. One great point in favour of Mr Atkinson's view is that it takes us so much further back. By it exogamy as a custom must have been much earlier than totemism, as at this stage the different group-families would not be distinguished by totem names; but its action as a law would become much stronger when reinforced by the totem superstitions, and would become fixed in rigid sexual taboos.[36] The strongest of these taboos is the avoidance between brothers and sisters; this is Mr Atkinson's *primal law*. It is a law that is still a working factor among barbarous races, and entails restrictions and avoidances of the most binding nature.

Unfortunately, I have not space to write even briefly on this important and deeply interesting subject. A right understanding of the whole question of sexual taboos, with the complicated totem superstitions on which they are based, is very necessary to any inquiry into the position of women. But to do this I should have to write another book. All I can say is this: these avoidances had in their origin no connection with the relative power of the two sexes; nor do I believe it can be proved that they were established by men rather than by women. They arose quite naturally, out of the necessity for regulation as a condition of peace.

Let me give one example that will serve to show how easily mistakes may arise. One of these rules, common among primitive peoples, prevents the women from eating with the men. This is often considered as a proof of the inferior position of the women, whereas it proves nothing of the kind. It is just one instance out of many numerous laws of avoidance between wife and husband, sister and brother, mother and son, and, indeed, between all relations in the family, which are part of the general rule to restrict sexual familiarity between the two sexes, set up at a time when moral restraints upon desire could act but feebly. It was only much later that these sexual taboos came to be fixed as superstitions, that with unbreakable fetters bound the freedom of women.

Here, indeed, are facts causing us to think. We perceive how old and strongly rooted are many customs from which today we are fighting to escape; customs of separation between women and men, which, with appalling conservatism, have descended through the ages. Will they ever be broken down? I do not know. These questions are not considered in adequate fashion; often we are ignorant of the deep forces driving the sexes into situations of antagonism. Clearly these primitive avoidances shed strong light on the sexual problems of our day. The subject is one of profound interest. I wish that it were possible to follow it, but all this lies outside the limit set to my inquiry, and already I have been led far from the patriarchal family.

The group has advanced in progress, and now has many features in common with existing savage peoples. The friendly conjunction of the father and his sons has established peace. Exogamy has begun to be practised; and the family in this way has been increased not only by the presence of the group-sons, but by their captured wives. We have seen that this would necessitate certain rules of sexual avoidance; thus the patriarch still holds marital rights over his wives and the group-daughters, while the captured women are sacred to the group-sons.

There is now a further important change to consider. Again the rights of the patriarch have to be restricted; a bar has to be raised to prevent his adding his daughters to his wives. Only by overcoming this habit of paternal incest can further social evolution become possible.

On this question I shall give the explanation of Mr Atkinson; and it is with real regret that the limit of my space makes it impossible to quote in full his own words.[37] The change came by *the entrance of outside suitors as husbands for the daughters and their acceptance as group-members.*

At this point a difficulty once again arises. By what means was the patriarch brought to accept the presence of these young intruders, thus usurping his sexual rights over his daughters? Mr Atkinson believes this could not have taken place during the life of the patriarch. "The initiative in change must have arisen irrespective of him, or without his presence." Here Mr Atkinson appears to me to fall into error, as once more he neglects to consider the effect of the young women's own desires. I hold that, by this time, the group-daughters, supported by their mothers, must have been strong enough to outwit their father (whose authority already had been weakened), if not openly, then by deceiving him. They would now see their brothers living with young wives. Is it credible, I ask, that they would remain content with the sexual embraces of their father?

In this connection it is of interest to note the opposition sometimes offered by young females to the advances of an old male among the families of monkeys. I have received quite recently an account of such a case in a letter from my friend, Max Henry Ferrass, formerly Inspector of Schools in India, and the author of a valuable work on Burmah. This is what he says —

"I once was able to observe a herd of common long-tailed monkeys of the Indian plains at play on a sandbank in a river. There were about fifty of all ages. There was one great bully among them who looked double the size of the average adult — and must have been double the weight, at any rate — whose sport was to chase the young females. They, knowing his game, fled before him, but he caught them readily. But before he could have his will of any, she would bound from his grasp as if stung, and always escape, as this sudden spurt of energy was more than he could control."

Here we have a clear instance in which the young females

escape from the thraldom of the male ruler of the horde. The power with which Mr Atkinson endows his human patriarch seems to me quite incredible. I have asserted again and again that the consolidation of the group-circle was of much greater importance to the women than to the men. Now this surely points to the acceptance of the view that the regulation of the brute sexual appetite was initiated by the women. Thereby, it may be pointed out, their action merely resembles womankind in any stage from the lowest degree of savagery to the highest stage of civilisation.

Moreover, there is further proof that points strongly to the acceptance of this view, that, the new departure, by which young husbands came into the group, was brought about by the women, in opposition to the knowledge and will of the patriarch. There exists a common custom among primitive tribes, which affords evidence of these outside suitors having visited their brides in secret. I refer to the practice by which intercourse between the husband and wife is carried on clandestinely by night. This is one of the earliest forms of marriage, and, further, it is closely connected, as I shall presently show, with the maternal family system. There appears to be no real cause for this precaution. I do not think it can be explained by the superstitious dread of the sexes for each other, expressing itself in this form of sexual taboo; as Mr Crawley and other writers suggest. Doubtless this is a factor, and a very powerful one, in the continuance of the custom, but it does not seem to me to be the true explanation of its origin. Such secrecy and clandestine meetings are, however, exactly what must have happened if the group-daughters received their lovers, as I would suggest, in defiance of the will of the patriarch. May not the custom as it still exists be a survival, retained and strengthened by superstition, from a time when these fugitive visits were necessary for safety?[38]

Mr Atkinson's view is different from mine. He does not allow any power at all to the women. He holds that after the death of the patriarch, his daughters, still young, would be left without husbands. To meet this difficulty suitors are brought from other groups by the brothers, *i. e.* the sons settled in the group and who now rule. We are asked to believe that they do this to relieve themselves of the maintenance of their widowed sisters, and to prevent their being captured and carried off to other groups. According to Mr Atkinson the presence of these outside lovers would not be dangerous to the family peace. They would come from neighbouring groups, from which the young men had already captured their wives. In this way the strangers would be the brothers of their women; and thus the brother-and-sister avoidance — the primal law already established — would prevent any fear of interference with the established marital rights on the part of the newcomers. I strongly differ from the suggestion that the brothers had to feed and maintain their widowed sisters; such an opinion is but another example of a failure to appreciate the women's side of the question. I allow willingly that the sisters may have had the assistance of their brothers; I incline, indeed, to the opinion that they would be strong enough to compel their help, though probably this was not necessary. The group-sisters and the group-brothers may well have united against the father, who was the enemy of both. To me the common-sense view is that these visits from outside suitors were first paid clandestinely at night. In the light of human nature it is at least probable that the tyrant father was deceived by his daughters and his sons. If already he was dead, what reason was there for any fear — why were the visits secret? This seems to show that I am right; that once more the initiative in the changes that led to regulation must be traced back to women. Afterwards, the custom thus established, would come to be recognised, and the practice of the husband visiting his wife by night would persist long after the danger making such secrecy necessary had ceased.

It will be readily seen that the introduction of young husbands from outside, by whatever means this was done, would be an immense gain in strength. Again, a new regulation in the sexual relationships would follow, and the group-daughters would now have husbands of their own generation, sacred to them. Furthermore, it was the first direct step in friendly union between group and group; a step that would open up ways to further progress. The husband, living in his own group, and visiting his wife in hers, would at once form a connecting link between two hitherto separate family circles, which friendly connection would not be broken, when, later, the custom arose of the husband leaving his group to take up his residence with his wife.

Such an arrangement must have been of immense advantage to the women. Under the new order, a wife married to one of these young strangers would hold a position of considerable power, that hitherto had been impossible. We have seen that the home was made by the group-women, and must have belonged to them; but so far, the continuance of a daughter in the home had entailed the acceptance of her father as a husband; the only way of escape being by capture, which — whether forced or, as I hold, aided by the girl's desire — sent her out from her own family as a stranger into a hostile group. Now this was reversed, and the husband entered as the alien into her home and family.

The following observation of Mr Atkinson in this connection must be quoted, as it is in strong agreement with my own view:

> As a wife who had not been captured, who, in fact, as an actual member of the group itself, was, so to speak, the capturer, *her position in regard to her dependent husband would be profoundly modified,* in comparison with that of the ordinary captive female, whereas such a captive, seised by the usual process of hostile capture, had been a mere chattel utterly without power; *she, as a free agent in her own home, with her will backed by that of her brothers*" [why not, I would ask, her sisters and her mother?] "*could impose law on her subject spouse.*[39]

In the foregoing sentences Mr Atkinson affirms the fateful significance to women of this new form of marriage. I am in wholehearted agreement with this opinion. I glean here and there from the wealth of Mr Atkinson's suggestions, statements which indicate how nearly he came to seeing all that I am trying to establish. Yet, I am compelled to disagree with his main argument; for always when he touches the woman's side, he falls back at once to consider the question in its relation to the males as the only important members in the group. I do not, for instance, accept his view that the captive wives were "mere chattels." They could not, under the conditions, have been without some considerable power, even if it arose only from the sexual dependence of their owners upon them. Much more significant, however, is Mr Atkinson's view regarding the authority of the wife in these new peaceable marriages. He sees one point only as arising from such a position, and finds "a psychological factor of enormous power, now for the first time able to make itself felt, in the play of sexual jealousy on the part of the wife." She would now "impose law on her subject spouse, and such law dictated by jealousy would ordain a bar to intercourse between him and her more youthful and hence more attractive daughters." Now, I do not deny that such a factor may have acted, for the incentive to jealousy arises always from individual as opposed to collective possession. Still I do not think jealousy can have been strong in this case, and, even if it were not, any reversion on the part of an alien father to the habits of the patriarch must have been impossible; such conduct would not have been tolerated by the other males in the group, nor by the daughters, now able to get young husbands for themselves. To limit the wife's power to this single issue can hardly be consistent with the conditions of the case. Mr Atkinson, in common with many other anthropologists, seems disposed to underrate the evidence regarding the far-reaching importance of this form of marriage. Among existing examples of the maternal family, the mother-rights and influences of women are dependent largely on the position of the husband as a stranger in her family home. This matter will become clear in the later part of my inquiry.

With the establishment of this new peaceful marriage the way was cleared for future progress; it is but a few further steps for the group to grow into the clan and the tribe. The family-group has increased greatly in size and in social organisation, from the time when it consisted of the patriarch, and his community of women and young children. The group-sons have brought in wives from other groups and have founded families; the group-daughters now have husbands who live with them. Primitive regulations over the marital rights have arisen, enabling peace to be maintained. Each family to some extent would be complete in itself. As the groups advanced in progress, totem names would come to be used as family marks of distinction, taken usually from some plant or animal. Peaceable marriages between the sons and daughters of the different groups would more and more become the habit, and would gradually take the place of capture marriages. The regulation of the sexual relationships, by which certain women and certain men became sacred to each other, would become more strongly fixed by custom; and afterwards the law would follow that a group of kindred, distinguished by its totem mark, might not marry within the hereditary name. The religious superstitions that came to be connected with these totem names would make binding the new order in the marriage law. When this stage was reached exogamy would be strictly practised; and in all cases under the complete maternal system, the woman on marriage would remain in her family home, where the husband would come to live with her as a kind of privileged guest.

There is one other matter that must be noted. The totem name was inherited from the mother, and not the father. This was the natural arrangement. When the group was small, there may have been a communal ownership of the group-children by the mothers, under the authority of the father. But this would not continue for long; when the group increased in numbers, the mother and her children would keep together as a little sub-family in the larger circle. This would be especially the case with captured wives, who would bring with them the totem marks of their groups, and this would be the name of the children. The naming of the children after the mother would also be the simplest way of distinguishing between the offspring of different wives, a distinction that would often be necessary, during the earlier conditions, among the polygamous fathers.

It is, however, an entirely mistaken view that the father's relation to the child was ever unrecognised. The taking of the name of the mother arose as a matter of course, and was adopted simply as being the most convenient custom. It is manifest that mother-descent has no connection with a period of promiscuity. Quite the reverse. All the conditions of mother-right arose out of the earliest movements towards order and regulation in the relationships of the sexes, and were not the result of licence. Nor was the naming of the child after the mother so much a question of relationship as of what may be called "social kinship." The causes which led to the maternal system are closely connected with the collective motive, which, if I am right, was in its origin, at least, the result of the union of the women against the selfish inclinations of the patriarch. When property rights came to be recognised, consisting at first of stores of food and the household goods, it would be perfectly natural that they should belong to the women, and descend through them. The inheritance would be to those most closely bound together, and who lived together in the same home. Thus it appears that descent through the mother was founded on social rights, by which the organisation of the family, such as membership in the group or clan, succession and inheritance were dependent on the mothers. In this sense, it is clear that the term mother-power is fully justified; it is nearer to the facts than the term mother-kin.

Further than this I must not go; the first part of my inquiry now has come to an end. It may seem to the reader that the patriarchal theory, in a book written to establish mother-right, has received more attention than was called for. I have discussed it so fully, not only because of the interest of the subject in proving the errors in the earlier theories of matriarchy, but because of the insight the conditions of the primordial group give us into the origin of the maternal family.

Many of the suggestions made are more or less hypothetical, but not a few, I think, are necessary deductions, based on what is most probable to have happened. I am fully aware of numerous omissions, and the inadequacy of this summary; but if the suggestions brought forward shall prove in themselves to have merit, it has seemed to me that a fruitful field of investigation has been opened. Much new ground had to be covered in this attempt to picture the position of women at a period so remote that the difficulties are very great. I hope at least to have cleared away the old errors, which connected mother-descent with uncertainty of paternity and an early period of promiscuity.

Recognising sexual jealousy as the moving force in brute man, I have accepted that the primeval family was of the patriarchal type. I have traced the probable development of the group-family, expanding by successive steps into larger groups living in peaceful association. In the earlier stage, whilst the men lived as solitary despots, the women enjoyed a communal life. It is thus probable that the leading power in the upward movement of the group developing into the clan and tribe arose among the united mothers, and not with the father. The women were forced into social conduct. On this belief is based the theory of mother-power.

The most important result we have gained is the proof that the maternal system was framed for order, and has no connection with sexual disorder. It is enough if I have suggested reasons to show that this widespread custom, which is practised still among many peoples, has nothing about it that is exceptional, nothing fantastic, nothing improbable. I hold it to be a perfectly natural arrangement — the practical outgrowth of the practical needs of primitive peoples. The strongest and the one certain claim for a belief in mother-right and mother-power must rest on this foundation. It is left for the second part of my book to prove how far I am right in what I claim.

The Mother-Age Civilisation

It's not too late to seek a newer world:
Tho' much is taken, much abides: and tho'
We are not now the strength which in old days
Moved earth and heaven, that which we are, we are;
One equal temper of heroic hearts;
Made weak by time and rule, but strong in will
To strive, to seek, to find, and not to yield.

— Tennyson

The Matriarchal Family among the American Indians

IT IS TIME now to turn to the actual subject of this investigation, in order to see how far the theory of mother-right has been helped by the lengthy examination of the patriarchal group.

Since the publication of *Das Mutterrecht* much has been written that has tended to raise doubts as to the soundness of the matriarchal theory, at least in the form held by its early supporters. A reaction in the opposite direction has set in, before which the former belief in mother-power has been transformed, and now seems likely to disappear altogether. In recent years, Westermarck, Starcke, Andrew Lang, N W Thomas, and Crawley among others have given utterance to this view. The prevalence of a system tracing descent through the mother is accepted by the majority of learned opinion, though it would seem somewhat grudgingly. Mr Crawley is the only writer, as far as I know, who denies that such a practice was ever common; the cases in which it still exists, as these cannot be denied, he regards as exceptions. He affirms: "There is no evidence that the maternal system was ever general or always preceded the paternal system." And again: "Though frequent, maternal descent cannot have been either universally or generally a stage through which man has passed."[40]

Mr Crawley considers this assumption may be taken for granted; so that he does not trouble himself about proofs. The subject of mother-right is dismissed as unworthy of serious attention. Such an attitude is surely instructive, and illustrates the failure, to which I have already pointed, in considering the woman's side in these questions. There would seem to be a tendency to doubt as being possible any family arrangement favourable to the authority of women. Even when descent through the mother is accepted as a phase in social development, it is denied that such descent confers any special rights to women.

One reason of this prejudice must be sought in the persistence of the puritan spirit: the objection to mother-kin rests mainly on the objection to loose sexual relationships. Thus it became necessary to attempt a new explanation of the origin of the custom, and hence my examination of the primordial patriarchal group. It may be thought that I should have done better to confine my inquiry to existing primitive peoples. But, if I am right, mother-power is rooted much further back than history, and arose first in the dawn of the human family. This had to be established.

It is clearly of vital importance to an inquiry that claims to set up a new belief in a discredited theory to protect it from those objections which hitherto have prevented its acceptance. This I have attempted to do. I have shown that the customs connected with mother-right had no connection at all with a state of promiscuity; that they were the result of order in the sexual relationships, and not of disorder. I have traced the causes which appear to have given rise to such a system, showing that the maternal order was not the first phase of the family, but was a natural forward movement — one which developed slowly and quite simply from the conditions of the patriarchal group. Moreover, I have maintained, and tried to prove, that the initiative in progress was taken by the women, they being inspired by their collective interest to overcome the individual interests of the male members of the group. If this is not assented to, then indeed, my view of mother-power can find no acceptance.

It is necessary, however, once more to guard against any mistake. I do not wish to prove a theory of gynaecocracy, or rule of woman. The title chosen for this chapter at once opens the way to misinterpretation. It might appear as if I supported Bachofen's supposition that, under a system of maternal descent women possessed supreme rule in the family and in the clan: this is a dream only of visionaries. I declare here that I consider the theory of the so-called matriarchate at once false and injurious: false, because it can lead to nothing; and injurious, because, while it cannot be supported by facts, it overthrows what can be proved by the evidence that is open to all investigators. Nothing will be gained by exaggeration and by claiming over much for women. The term "matriarchal" takes too much for granted that women at one period ruled. Such a view is far from the truth. All I claim, then, is this: the system by which the descent of the name and the inheritance of property passes through the female side of the family placed women in a favourable position, with definite rights in the family and clan, rights which, in some cases, resulted in their having great and even extraordinary power. This, I think, may be granted. *If descent through the father stands, as it is held to do, for the predominance of man over woman — the husband over the wife, then it is at least surely possible that descent through the mother may in some cases have stood for the predominance of the wife over the husband.* The reader will judge how far the examples of the maternal family I am able to bring forward support this claim.

The evidence for mother-right has never yet been fully brought into notice; but much of the evidence is now available. Our knowledge of the customs of primitive peoples has increased greatly of late years, and these afford a wide field for inquiry. And although the examples of the complete maternal family existing today are few in number — probably not more than twenty tribes,[41] yet the important fact is that they occur among widely separated peoples in all the great regions of the uncivilised world. Moreover, side by side with these, are found a much larger number of imperfect systems, which give unmistakable evidence of an earlier maternal stage. Such examples are specially instructive; they belong to a transitional period, and show the maternal family in its decline as it passes into a new patriarchal stage; often, indeed, we see the one system competing in conflict with the other.

In this connection I may note that Westermarck does not accept an early period when descent was traced exclusively through the mother; he gives a long list of peoples among whom the system is not practised. These passages occur in his well-known *Criticism of the Hypothesis of Promiscuity*,[42] and his whole argument is based on the assumption that mother-right arose through the tie between the father and the child being unrecognised. But mother-descent has no connection at all with uncertainty of paternity. I venture to think Dr Westermarck has not sufficiently considered this aspect of the question, and, if I mistake not, it is this confusion of mother-descent with promiscuity which explains his attitude towards the maternal system, and his failure to recognise its favourable influence on the status of women. In his opinion this system of tracing descent does not materially affect the relative power of the two sexes.[43] In such a view I cannot help thinking he is mistaken; and I am supported in this by the fact that he makes the important qualification that the husband's power is impaired when he lives among his wife's kinsfolk. Now, it is this form of marriage, or the more primitive custom when the husband only visits his wife, that is practised among the peoples who have preserved the complete maternal family. Under such a domestic arrangement, which really reverses the position of the wife and the husband, mother-right is found; this maternal marriage is, indeed, the true foundation of the woman's power. Where the marriage system has been changed from the maternal to the paternal form, and the wife is taken from the protection of her own kindred to live in the home of her husband, even when descent is still traced through the mother, the chief authority is almost always in the hands of the father. Thus it need not cause surprise to find mother-descent combined with a fully established patriarchal rule. But among such peoples practices may often be met with that can be explained only as survivals from an earlier maternal system. Moreover, in other cases, we meet with tribes that have not yet advanced to the maternal stage. A study of existing tribes, and of the records of ancient civilisations, will yield any number of examples.

Unmistakable traces of mother-right may, indeed, be found by those, whose eyes are opened to see, in all races. In peasant festivals and dances, and in many religious beliefs and ceremonies, we may meet with such survivals. They may be traced in our common language, especially in the words used for sex and for kin relationships. We can also find them shadowed in certain of our marriage rites, and sex habits today. Another source of evidence is furnished by the widespread early occurrence of mother-goddesses, who must be connected with a system which places the mother in the forefront of religious thought. Further proof may be gathered from folk stories and heroic legends, whose interest offers rich rewards in suggestions of a time when honour rested with the sex to whom the inheritance belonged. Thus, the difficulty of establishing a claim for mother-right and mother-power does not rest in any paucity of proof — but rather in its superabundance.

It would be superfluous for me to dwell on the difficulties of such an inquiry. The subject is immensely complicated and wide-reaching, so that I must keep strictly to the path set before me. It is my purpose to outline the domestic relations in the maternal family clan, and to examine the sex-customs and forms of marriage. I shall limit myself to those matters which throw some light on the position of women, and shall touch on the features of social life only in so far as they illustrate this. These questions will be discussed in the three succeeding chapters. Some portion of the matter given has appeared already in the section on the "Mother-Age Civilisation" in *The Truth about Woman*, which gives examples of the maternal family in America, Australia, India and other countries. Such examples formed a necessary part of the historical section of that work; they are even more necessary to this inquiry. Many new examples will be given, and the examination of the whole subject will be more exhaustive. These chapters will be followed by a discussion of certain difficulties, and an examination of the transition period in which the maternal family gave way to the second patriarchal stage with the family founded on the authority of the father. A short chapter will be devoted to the work done by women in primitive tribes and its importance in relation to their position. Then will come as full an account as is possible of the traces of the mother-age to be found in the records of ancient and existing civilised races; while a brief chapter will be added on certain myths and legends which help to elucidate the theory of women's early power. The final chapter will treat of general conclusions, with an attempt to suggest certain facts which seem to bear on present-day problems. Throughout I shall support my investigation (as far as can be done in a work primarily designed for a textbook) by examples, which, in each case, have been carefully chosen from trustworthy evidence of those who are personally acquainted with the habits of the peoples of whom they write. I shall try to avoid falling into the error of a one-sided view. Facts will be more important than reflections, and as far as possible, I shall let these speak for themselves.

Let us now concentrate our attention on the complete maternal family, where the clan is grouped around the mothers.

The examples in this chapter will be taken from the aboriginal tribes of North and South America among whom traces of the maternal system are common, while in some cases mother-right is still in force. At the period of European discovery the American Indians were already well advanced in the primitive arts, and were very far removed from savagery. Their domestic and social habits showed an organisation of a very remarkable character; among certain tribes there was a communal maternal family, interesting and complicated in its arrangements. Such customs had prevailed from an antiquity so remote that their origin seems to have been lost in the obscurity of the ages. It is possible, however, to see how this communism in living may have arisen and developed out of the conditions we have studied in the far distant patriarchal groups. For this reason they afford a very special interest to our inquiry.

Morgan, who was commissioned by the American Government

to report on the customs of the aboriginal inhabitants, gives a description of the system as it existed among the Iroquois:

> Each household was made up on the principle of kin. The married women, usually sisters, own or collateral, were of the same *gens* or clan, the symbol or *totem* of which was often painted upon the house, while their husbands and the wives of their sons belonged to several other *gentes*. The children were of the *gens* of their mother. As a rule the sons brought home their wives, and in some cases the husbands of the daughters were admitted to the maternal household. Thus each household was composed of persons of different *gentes*, but the predominating number in each household would be of the same *gens*, namely, that of the mother.[44]

We see here, at once, the persistence and development of the conditions and later customs of the patriarchal family-group, now evolved into the clan. In the far-distant days the jealous spirit was still strong; now it has been curbed and regulated, and the female yoke binds the clan together. We have the mothers as the centre of the communal home; the sons bringing their wives to live in the circle, while the daughters' husbands are received as permanent guests. Under such a system the mothers are related to each other, and belong to the same clan, and their children after them; the fathers are not bound together by the same ties and are of different clans. The limits within which marriage can take place are fixed, and we can trace the action of the ancient primal law in the bar that prohibits the husband from being of the same clan as his wife. Though the husband takes up his abode in the wife's family, dwelling there *during her life and his good behaviour,*[45] he still belongs to his own family. The children of the marriage are of the kindred of the mother, and never of his kindred: they are lost to his family. Thus there can be no extension of the clan through the males, it is the wife's clan that is extended by marriage.[46]

The important point to note is that the conditions of the clan are still favourable to the social conduct of the women, who are attached much more closely to the home and to each other than can be the case with the men. The wife never leaves the home, because she is considered the mistress, or, at least, the heiress. In the house all the duties and the honour as the head of the household fall upon her. This position may be illustrated by the wife's obligation to her husband and his family, which are curiously in contrast with what is usually expected from a woman. Thus a wife is not only bound to give food to her husband, to cook his provisions when he sets out on expeditions, but she has likewise to assist members of his family when they cultivate their fields, and to provide wood for an allotted period for the use of his family. In this work she is assisted by women of her clan. The women are also required in case of need to look after their parents.

There are many interesting customs in the domestic life of the Iroquois. I can notice a few only. The system of living, at the time Morgan visited the tribes, consisted of a plan at once novel and distinctive. Each *gens* or clan lived in a long tenement house, large enough to accommodate the separate families. These houses were erected on frames of poles, covered with bark, and were from fifty to a hundred feet in length. A passage way led down the centre, and rooms were portioned off on either side: the doors were at each end of the passage. An apartment was allotted to each family. There were several fireplaces, usually one for every four families, which were placed in the central passage: there were no chimneys. The Iroquois lived in these long houses, *Ho-de-no-sau-nee*, up to AD 1700, and in occasional instances for a hundred years later. They were not peculiar to the Iroquois, but were used by many tribes. Unfortunately this wise plan of living has now almost entirely passed away.

I wish that I had space to give a fuller account of these families.[47] Each household practised communism in living, and made a common stock of the provisions acquired by fishing and hunting, and by the cultivation of maize and plants. The curse of individual accumulation would seem not to have existed. Ownership of land and all property was held in common. Each household was directed by the matron who supervised its domestic economy. After the daily meal was cooked at the several fires, the matron was summoned, and it was her duty to apportion the food from the kettle to the different families according to their respective needs. What food remained was placed in the charge of another woman until it was required by the matron. In this connection Mr Morgan says: "This plan of life shows that their domestic economy was not without method, and it displays the care and management of women, low down in barbarism, for husbanding their resources and for improving their conditions."

In this statement, made by one who was intimately acquainted with the customs of this people there is surely confirmation of what I have claimed for women? The further we go in our inquiry the more we are driven to the conclusion that the favourable conditions uniting the women with one another exerted a powerful influence on their character. I think this is a view of the maternal family system that has never received its proper meed of attention.

It must be noted that the women did not eat with the men; but the fact that the apportioning of the food was in the women's hands is sufficient proof that this separation of women and men, common among most primitive peoples, has no connection with the superiority of one sex over the other. It is interesting to find that only one prepared meal was served in each day. But the pots were always kept boiling over the fires, and any one who was hungry, either from the household or from any other part of the village, had a right to order it to be taken off and to eat as he or she pleased.

We may notice the influence of their communistic living in all the Indian customs. At all times the law of hospitality was strictly observed. Food was dispensed in every case to those who needed it; no excuse was ever made to avoid giving. If through misfortune one household fell into want, the needs were freely supplied from the stock laid by for future use in another household. Hunger and destitution could not exist in any part of an Indian village or encampment while plenty prevailed elsewhere. Such generosity at a time when food was often difficult to obtain, and its supply was the first concern of life, is a remarkable fact. Nor does this generosity seem, as might be thought, to have led to idleness and improvidence. He who begged, when he could work, was stigmatised with the disgraceful name of "poltroon" or "beggar"; but the miser who refused to assist his neighbour was branded as "a bad character." Mr Morgan, commenting on this phase of the Indian life says: "I much doubt if the civilised world would have in their institutions any system which can properly be called more humane and charitable."

These reflections induce one to ask: What were the causes of this humane system of living among a people considered as uncivilised? Now, I do not wish to claim overmuch for women. We have seen, however, that the control and distribution of the supply of food was placed in the hands of the matrons, thus their association with the giving of food must be accepted. Is not this fact sufficient to indicate the reason that made possible this communism? To me it is plain that these remarkable institutions were connected with the maternal family, in which the collective interests were more considered than is possible in a patriarchal society, based upon individual inclination and proprietary interests.

A brief notice must now be given to the system of government. An Indian tribe was composed of several *gentes* or clans, united in what is known as a *phratry* or brotherhood. The tribe was an assemblage of the *gentes*. The *phratry* among the Iroquois was organised partly for social and partly for religious objects. Each *gens* was ruled by chiefs of two grades, distinguished by Morgan as the *sachem* and common chiefs. The *sachem* was the official head of the *gens*, and was elected by its adult members, male and female. The *sachems* and chiefs claimed no superiority and were never more than the exponents of the popular will of the people. Unanimity among the *sachems* was required on all public questions. This was the fundamental law of the brotherhood; if all efforts failed to gain agreement the matter in question was dropped. Under such a system individual rule or the power of one *gens* over the other became impossible. All the members of the different *gentes* were personally free; equal in privileges, and in position, and in rights. "Liberty, equality, and fraternity," though never formulated, were the cardinal principles of the *gens*.[48] Mr Morgan holds the opinion that "this serves to explain that sense of independence and personal dignity universally attributed to the Indian character."

Regarding the part taken by the women in the government, we have very remarkable testimony. Schoolcraft,[49] in his elaborate study of the customs of the Indian tribes, states that the women had "a conservative power in the political deliberations. The matrons had their representatives in the public councils, and they exercised a negative, or what we call a veto, power, in the important question of the declaration of war." They had also the right to interpose in bringing about a peace. Heriot also affirms: "In the women is vested the foundation of all real authority. They give efficiency to the councils and are the arbiters of war and peace.... It is also to their disposal that the captured slaves are committed." And again: "Although by custom the leaders are chosen from among the men, and the affairs which concern the tribe are settled by a council of ancients, it would yet seem that they only represented the women, and assisted in the discussion of subjects which principally related to that sex."[50]

These remarkable social and domestic conditions were common to the American Indians under the maternal system. The direct influence of women, as directors through the men, is a circumstance of much interest. Among the Senecas, an Iroquoian tribe with the complete maternal family, the authority was very certainly in the hands of the women. Morgan quotes an account of their family system, given by the Rev Ashur Wright for many years a resident among the Senecas, and familiar with their language and customs.

> As to their family system, it is probable that one clan predominated (in the houses), the women taking in husbands,

however, from other clans, and sometimes for novelty, some of their sons bringing in their young wives, until they felt brave enough to leave their mothers. Usually the female portion ruled the house, and were doubtless clannish enough about it. The stores were in common, but woe to the luckless husband or lover who was too shiftless to do his share of the providing. No matter how many children or whatever goods he might have in the house, he might at any time be ordered to pack up his blanket and budge, and after such orders it would not be healthful for him to attempt to disobey; the house would be too hot for him, and unless saved by the intercession of some aunt or grandmother, he must retreat to his own clan, or, as was often done, go and start a new matrimonial alliance in some other. The women were the great power among the clans as everywhere else. They did not hesitate, when occasion required, to 'knock off the horns,' as it was technically called, from the head of a chief and send him back to the ranks of the warrior. The original nomination of the chief also always rested with them.

Mr Morgan affirms his acceptance of the Indian women's authority, and says, after quoting this passage: "The mother-right and gynaecocracy among the Iroquois here plainly indicated is not over-drawn. The mothers and their children, as we have seen, were of the same *gens*, and to them the household belonged. The position of the mother was eminently favourable to her influence in the household, and tended to strengthen the maternal bond."[51]

It is important to note that among the Iroquois polygamy is not permitted, nor does it appear ever to be practised. Many instances are reported in the Seneca tribe of a woman having more than one husband, but an Iroquoian man is never allowed more than one wife.[52] This is the more remarkable when we consider the fact that the mothers nurse their children for a very long period, during which time they do not cohabit with their husbands. Such entire absence of polygamy is to be explained, in part, by the maternal marriage, a system which in its origin was closely connected with sexual regulation; nor would plurality of wives be possible in a society in which all the members of both sexes enjoyed equal privileges, and were in a position of absolute equality. Marriages usually take place at an early age. Under the maternal form, the husband living with the wife worked for her family, and commonly gained his footing only through his service. As suitor he was required to make presents to the bride's family. During the first year of marriage all the produce of his hunting expeditions belonged to the wife, and afterwards he shared his goods equally with her. The marriages were negotiated by the mothers: sometimes the father was consulted, but this was little more than a compliment, as his approbation or opposition was usually disregarded. Often it was customary for the bridegroom to seek private interviews at night with his betrothed; clearly a survival from a time when such secrecy in love was necessary. In some instances it was enough if the suitor went and sat by the girl's side in her apartment; if she permitted this, and remained where she was, it was taken for consent, and the act would suffice for marriage. Girls were allowed the right of choice in the selection of their partners. There is abundant testimony as to the happiness of the marriage state. Divorce was, however, allowed by mutual consent, and was carried out without dispute, quarrel or contradiction.[53] If a husband and a wife could not agree, they parted amicably, or two unhappy pairs would exchange husbands and wives. An early French missionary remonstrated with a couple on such a transaction, and was told: "My wife and I could not agree; my neighbour was in the same case, so we exchanged wives and all four were content. What can be more reasonable than to render one another mutually happy, when it costs so little, and does nobody any harm."[54] It would seem that these maternal peoples have solved many difficulties of domestic and social life better than we ourselves have done.

The Wyandots, another Iroquoian tribe, maintained the maternal household, though they seem to have reached a later stage of development than the Senecas. They camped in the form of a horseshoe, every clan together in regular order. Marriage between members of the same clan was forbidden; the children belonged to the clan of the mother. The husbands retained all their rights and privileges in their own *gentes,* though they lived in the *gentes* of their wives. After marriage the pair resided, for a time, at least, with the wife's mother, but afterwards they set up housekeeping for themselves.[55]

We may note in this change of residence the creeping in of changes which inevitably led in time to the decay of the maternal family and the reassertion of the patriarchal authority of the father. This is illustrated further by the Musquakies, also belonging to the Algonquian stock. Though still organised in clans, descent is no longer reckoned through the mother; the bridegroom, however, serves his wife's family, and he lives in her home. This does not make him of her clan, but she belongs to his, till his death or divorce separates her from him. As for the children, the minors at the termination of the marriage belong to the mother's clan, but those who had had the puberty feast are counted to the father's clan.[56]

The male authority was felt chiefly in periods of war. This may be illustrated by the Wyandots, who have an elaborate system of government. In each *gens* there is a small council composed of four women, called *yu-waí-yu-wá-na;* chosen by the heads of the household. These women select a chief of the *gens* from its male members, that is, from their brothers and sons. He is the head of the *gentile* council. The council of the tribe is composed of the aggregated *gentile* councils; and is thus made up of four-fifths of women and one-fifth of men. The *sachem* of the tribes, or tribal chief, is chosen by the chiefs of the *gentes.* All the civil government of the *gens* and of the tribe is carried on by these councils; and as the women so largely outnumbered the men, who are also — with the one exception of the tribal chief — chosen by them, it is evident that the social government of the *gens* and tribe is largely controlled by them. On military affairs, however, the men have the direct authority, though, as has been stated, the women have a veto power and are "allowed to exercise a decision in favour of peace." There is a military council of all the able-bodied men of the tribe, with a military chief chosen by the council.[57] This seems a very wise adjustment of civic duties; the constructive social work and the maintaining of peace directed by the women; the destructive work of war in the hands of men.

Powell gives an interesting account of their communal life. Each clan owns its own lands which it cultivates; but within these lands each household has its own patch. It is the women councillors who partition the clan lands among the households. The partition takes place every two years. But while each household has its own patch of ground, the cultivation is communal; that is, all the able-bodied women of the clan take a share in cultivating every patch. Each clan has a right to the service of all its women in the cultivation of the soil. It would be difficult to find a more striking example than this of communism in labour. I claim it as proof of what I have stated in an earlier chapter of the conditions driving women into combination and social conduct.

If we turn now to the South American continent we shall find many interesting survivals of the complete maternal family, in particular among the Pueblo peoples of New Mexico and Arizona, so called from the Spanish word *pueblo*, a town. The customs of the people have been carefully studied and recorded by Bancroft, Schoolcraft, Morgan, Tylor, McGee, the Spanish historian, Herrera, and other travellers. When first visited by European anthropologists the country was divided into provinces, and in many provinces the people lived in communities or little republics. The communal life was here more developed even than among the Northern Indians. The people lived together in joint tenement houses, much larger, and of more advanced architecture, than the long houses of the Iroquois. These houses are constructed of adobe, brick and stone, imbedded in mortar; one house will contain as many as 50, 100, 200, and in some cases, 500 apartments. Speaking of these houses, Bancroft states: "The houses are common property, and both women and men assist in building them; the men erect the wooden frames, and the women make the mortar and build the walls. In place of lime for mortar they mix ashes with earth and charcoal. They make *adobes*, or sun-dried bricks, by mixing ashes and earth with water."[58] Cushing, who visited and lived with the Zuñi Indians, records that among them the houses are entirely built by the women, the men supplying the material. These houses are erected in terrace form; within they are provided with windows, fireplaces and chimneys, and the entrance to the different apartments is gained by rude pole ladders. The pueblo, or village, consists of one or two, or sometimes a greater number of these houses, each containing a hundred or more families, according to the number of apartments.

Among the Creek Indians of Georgia, Morgan recounts a somewhat different mode of communal dwelling as formerly being practised. In 1790 they were living in small houses, placed in clusters of from four to eight together; and each cluster forming a *gens* or clan, who ate and lived in common. The food was prepared in one hut, and each family sent for its portion. The smallest of these "garden cities" contained 10 to 40 groups of houses, the largest from 50 to 200.[59] These communistic dwelling-houses are so interesting and so important that I would add a few words. Here, we have among these maternal peoples a system of living which appears to be identical with the improved conditions of associated dwelling now beginning to be tried. How often we consider new things that really are very old! In the light of these examples, our co-operative dwelling-houses and garden cities can no longer be regarded as experiments. They were in use in the mother-age, when many of our new (!) ideas seem to have been common. Can this be because of the extended power held by women, who are more practical and careful of detail than men are? I believe that it is possible. This would explain, too, the revival of the same ideas today, when women are taking up their part again in social life. To those who are questioning the waste and discomfort of our solitary homes I would recommend a careful study of this primitive communism. I would point out the connection of the social ideal with the maternal family, while the home that is solitary and unsocial must be regarded as having arisen from the patriarchal customs. I have had occasion again and again to note that collective interests are more considered by women; and individual interests by men. This, at least, is how I see it; and a study of the Indian maternal families seems to give confirmation to such a conclusion.

But to return to the Pueblo peoples. The tribes are divided into exogamous totem clans. Kinship is reckoned through the women, and in several tribes we find the complete maternal family. Among such peoples the husband goes to live with the wife and becomes an inmate of her family. If the house is not large enough, additional rooms are built on to the communal home and connected with those already occupied. Hence a family with many daughters increases, while one consisting of sons dies out.

The marriage customs and relationships between the young men and the girls are instructive; they vary in the different tribes, but have some points in common. The Pueblos are monogamists, and polygamy is not allowed amongst them. Bancroft records a very curious custom. The morals of the young people are carefully guarded by a kind of secret police, whose duty it is to report all irregularities; and in the event of such taking place the young man and the girl are compelled to marry.[60] Now, whatever opinion may be held of such interference with the lovemaking of the young people, it affords strong proof of the error which has hitherto connected the maternal system with unregulated sexual relationships. This is a fact I am again and again compelled to point out, risking the fear of wearying the reader.

Among some tribes freedom is permitted to the women before marriage. Heriot states that the natives who allow this justify the custom, and say "that a young woman is mistress of her own person, and a free agent."[61] The tie of marriage is, however, observed more strictly than among many civilised monogamous races. And this is so, although divorce is always easy and by mutual consent; a couple being able to separate at once if they are dissatisfied with each other. Here are facts that may well cause us to think. As for the courtship, the usual custom is reversed; when a girl is disposed to marry she does not wait for a young man to propose to her, but selects one to her liking, and then consults her family as to his suitability as a husband. The suitor has to serve the bride's family before he can be accepted, and in some cases the conditions are binding and exceedingly curious.

How simple and really beautiful are the conditions of life among these people may be seen from the idyllic record of the Zuñi Indians given by Mr Cushing.[62] He describes how the Zuñi girl, when taking a fancy to a young man, conveys a present of thin *hewe*-bread to him as a token, and becomes his affianced, or as they say "his-to-be." He then sews clothes and moccasins for her, makes her a necklace of gay beads, and combs her hair out on the terrace in the sun. After his term of service is over, and all is settled, he takes up his residence with her; then the married life begins. "With the woman rests the security of the marriage tie, and, it must be said, in her high honour, that she rarely abuses the privilege; that is, never sends her husband 'to the home of his fathers' unless he richly deserves it." Divorce is by mutual consent, and a husband and wife would "rather separate than live together unharmoniously." This testimony is confirmed by Mrs Stevenson, who visited the Zuñis, and writes with enthusiasm of the people. "Their domestic life might well serve as an example for the civilised world. They do not have large families. The husband and wife are deeply attached to one another and to their children." "The keynote of this harmony is the supremacy of the wife in the home. The house with all that is in it is hers, descending to her through her mother from a long line of ancestresses; and the husband is merely her permanent guest. The children — at least the female children — have their share in the common home; the father has none." "Outside the house the husband has some property in the fields, although in earlier times he had no possessory rights and the land was held in common. Modern influences have reached the Zuñi, and mother-right seems to have begun its inevitable decay."[63]

The Hopis, another Pueblo tribe, are more conservative, and

with them the women own all the property except the horses and donkeys, which belong to the men. Among the Pueblos the women commonly have control over the granary, and they are very provident about the future. Ordinarily they try to have one year's provisions on hand. It is only when two years of scarcity succeed each other that the community suffers hunger. Like the Zuñis, the Hopis are monogamists. Sexual freedom is, however, permitted to a girl before marriage. This in no way detracts from her good repute; even if she has given birth to a child "she will be sure to marry later on, unless she happens to be shockingly ugly." Nor does the child suffer, for among these maternal peoples, the bastard takes an equal place with the child born in wedlock. The bride lives for the first few weeks with her husband's family, during which time the marriage takes place, the ceremony being performed by the bridegroom's mother, whose family also provides the bride with her wedding outfit. The couple then return to the home of the wife's parents, where they remain, either permanently, or for some years, until they can obtain a separate dwelling. The husband is always a stranger, and is so treated by his wife's kin. The dwelling of his mother remains his true home, in sickness he returns to her to be nursed, and stays with her until he is well again. Often his position in his wife's home is so irksome that he severs his connection with her and her family, and returns to his old home. On the other hand, it is not uncommon for the wife, should her husband be absent, to place his goods outside the door: an intimation which he well understands, and does not intrude upon her again.[64]

Again, among the Pueblo peoples, we may consider the Sai. Like the other tribes they are divided into exogamous totem clans; descent is traced only through the mother. The tribe through various reasons has been greatly reduced in numbers, and whole clans have died out, and under these circumstances exogamy has ceased to be strictly enforced. This has led to other changes. The Sai are still normally monogamous. When a young man wishes to marry a girl he speaks first to her parents; if they are willing he addresses himself to her. On the day of the marriage he goes alone to her home, carrying his presents wrapped in a blanket, his mother and father having preceded him thither. When the young people are seated together the parents address them in turn, enjoining unity and forbearance. This constitutes the ceremony. Tribal custom requires the bridegroom to reside with the wife's family.[65]

All the Pueblo peoples are more advanced than the greater number of the neighbouring tribes; their matrimonial customs are more refined, their domestic life much happier, and they have an appreciation of love, a rare thing in primitive peoples.[66] Among other tribes purchase of a wife is common, always a sure sign of the enslavement of women. Thus in Columbia what is most prised in a woman is her aptitude for labour, and the price paid for her (usually in horses) depends on her capacity as a beast of burden. Sometimes, as in California, a suitor obtains a wife on credit, but then the man is called "half married;" and until her price is paid he has to labour as a slave for her parents. Here, as elsewhere, morality is simply a custom of habit; Bancroft says that purchase of a wife has become accepted as honourable, so that among the Californian Redskins "the children of a wife who has cost nothing to her husband are looked down upon."[67] Such customs are in sharp contrast to the liberty granted to the woman among the Pueblos. As an example of women's power carried to the limit of tyranny, we may note the Nicaraguans, of whom Bancroft states that "the husbands are said to have been so much under the control of their wives that they were obliged to do the housework, while the women attended to the trading." Under these circumstances it is perhaps not surprising to find the women described as "great shrews, who would on the slightest provocation drive their offending husbands out of the house."[68] This is a curious case of the despotic rule of women. Westermarck accounts for their position by the strict monogamy that is enforced, but I do not think this can be the true explanation.[69]

Among the Guanas the women make their own stipulations with their lovers before marriage, arranging what they are to do in the household. They are also said to decide the conditions of the marriage, whether it is to be monogamous, or if polygamy or polyandry is to be allowed.[70] The Zapotecs and other tribes inhabiting the Isthmus of Tehuantepec, are remarkable for "the gentleness, affection, and frugality that characterises the marital relations. Polygamy is not permitted, which is very remarkable as the women greatly outnumber the men."[71]

Lastly, I wish to bring forward a very striking example of the complete maternal family among the Seri Indians, on the south-west coast of North America, now reduced to a single tribe. Their curious and interesting marriage customs have been described by McGee, who visited the people to report on their customs for the American Government. The Seri are probably the most primitive tribe in the American continent. At the time of Mr McGee's visit they preserved the maternal system in its early form, and are therefore an instructive example by which to estimate the position of the women.[72]

> The tribe is divided into exogamous totem clans. Marriage is arranged exclusively by the women. The elder woman of the suitor's family carries the proposal to the girl's clan mother. If this is entertained, the question of marriage is discussed at length by the matrons of the two clans. The girl herself is consulted; a *jacal* is erected for her, and after many deliberations, the bridegroom is provisionally received into the wife's clan for a year under conditions of the most exacting character. He is expected to prove his worthiness of a permanent relationship by demonstrating his ability as a provider, and by showing himself an implacable foe to aliens. He is compelled to support all the female relatives of his bride's family by the products of his skill and industry in hunting and fishing for one year. There is also another provision of a very curious nature. The lover is permitted to share the *jacal*, or sleeping-robe, provided for the prospective matron by her kinswomen, not as a privileged spouse, but merely as a protective companion; and throughout this probationary time he is compelled to maintain continence

— he must display the most indubitable proof of his moral force.

This test of the Seri lover must not mistakenly be thought to be connected, as might appear, with the modern idea of continence. As is pointed out by McGee, it arose out of the primitive sexual taboos, and is imposed on the young man as a test of his strength to abstain from any sexual relationships outside the proscribed limits. Such a moral test may once have been common, but seems to have been lost except among the Seri; though a curious vestige appears in the anti-nuptial treatment of the bridegroom, in the Salish tribe. The material test is common among many peoples, and must not be confused with the later custom of payment for the wife by presents given to her family. Still this Seri marriage is one of the most curious I know among any primitive peoples. And the continence demanded from the bridegroom appears more extraordinary if we compare it with the freedom granted to the bride. "During this period the always dignified position occupied by the daughters of the house culminates." Among other privileges she is allowed to receive the "most intimate attentions from the clan-fellows of the group." "She is the receiver of the supplies furnished by her lover, measuring his competence as would-be husband. Through his energy she is enabled to dispense largess with a lavish hand, and thus to dignify her clan and honour her spouse in the most effective way known to primitive life; and at the same time she enjoys the immeasurable moral stimulus of realising she is the arbiter of the fate of a man who becomes a warrior or an outcast at her bidding, and through him of the future of two clans — she is raised to a responsibility in both personal and tribal affairs which, albeit temporary, is hardly lower than that of the warrior chief." At the close of the year, if all goes well, the probation ends in a feast provided by the lover, who now becomes the husband, and finally enters his wife's *jacal* as "consort-guest." His position is wholly subordinate, and without any authority whatever, either over his children or over the property. In his mother's hut he has rights, which seem to continue after his marriage, but in his wife's hut he has none.

I have now collected together, with as much exactitude as I could, what is known of the maternal family in the American continents. There are many tribes in which descent is reckoned through the father, and it would be bold to assert that these have all passed through the maternal stage. An examination of their customs shows, in some cases, survivals, which point to such conclusion; among other tribes it seems probable that the maternal clan has not developed. As illustrations of mother-power, I claim the examples given speak for themselves. It may, of course, be urged that these complete maternal families are exceptions, and thus to dismiss them as unimportant. But this is surely an unscientific way of settling the question. One has to accept these cases, or to prove that they are untrue. Moreover, I have by no means exhausted the evidence; and to these complete maternal families might be added examples from other tribes which would furnish similar proofs, but there is such consistency of custom among them all that further accounts may be dispensed with.

There is one other matter for which I would claim attention before closing this chapter on the American Indians, and that is the remarkable similarity to be noticed in many tribes between the faces of the men and the women. To me this is a point of deep interest, though I do not claim to understand it. My attention was first drawn to notice this likeness between the two sexes when I came to know some Iroquois natives who live in England. I was at once struck with the appearance of the men: though strong and powerfully built, they were strikingly like women. Since then I have examined many portraits of the North Indian tribes; I have found that the great majority of men approach much more nearly to the feminine than the male type. I might, however, hesitate to bring the matter forward, were it founded only on my own observation. But in my reading I have found an important reference to the question in a recent work, "The Indians of North America in Recent Times," by Mr Cyrus Thomas, PhD, archaeologist in the *Bureau of American Ethnology*.

He writes as follows (p 41):

> Another curious fact, which has not hitherto received special notice, though apparently of considerable interest, is the prevailing feminine physiognomy of the males, at least of those of the northern section. If any one will take the trouble to study carefully a hundred or more good photographs of males of pure blood he will find that two thirds, if not a greater proportion, show feminine faces. The full significance of this fact is not apparent, but it seems to bear to some extent upon the question of the evolution of the race.

What this fact suggests is a problem to which it is very difficult even to guess at an answer. Does this lack of differentiation in the physiognomy of the Indians point to something much deeper? Are the men really like the women? Such a conception opens up considerations of very great significance. So far as I understand the matter, it appears that, as well as the deep inherent differences between the two sexes, there are other differences due to divergence in function. It seems probable that changes in environment or in function (as when one sex, for some reason or other, performs the duties usually undertaken by the other sex), may alter or modify the differences which tend to thrust the sexes apart. I feel very sure that there can be changes in the secondary sexual characters of the male and female. This is sufficiently proved by many examples. Can we, then, accept the theory that an environment, which favours women's forceful function, may modify the infinitely complicated characters of sex, which, as yet, we so imperfectly understand? I do not know with any certainty. Yet I can see no other interpretation; and, if I mistake not, it may be possible in this way to cast a light on one of the most difficult problems with which we are faced today.

The Maternal Family among the Khasis

THERE ARE, PERHAPS, no people among whom the family in the full maternal form can be studied with more advantage than the Khasi Hill tribes, in the north-east of India. This race has a special interest as a people who, in modern times, have preserved their independence and their ancestral customs through many centuries. We find mother-descent strictly practised, combined with great and even extraordinary rights on the part of the women. The isolation of the Khasis may account for this conservatism, but, as will appear later, there are other causes to explain the freedom and power of the Khasi women. We are fortunate in having a fuller knowledge of the Khasi tribes, than is common of many primitive peoples. Their institutions and interesting domestic customs have been carefully noted by ethnologists and travellers, and in all accounts there is united testimony to the high status of the women. I will quote a statement of Sir Charles Lyell,[73] which affirms this fact very strongly:

> Their social organisation presents one of the most perfect examples still surviving of matriarchal institutions carried out with a logic and a thoroughness which, to those accustomed to regard the status and authority of the father as the foundation of society, are exceedingly remarkable. Not only is the mother the head and source and only bond of union of the family, in

> the most primitive part of the hills, the Synteng country, she is the only owner of real property, and through her alone is inheritance transmitted. The father has no kinship with his children, who belong to their mother's clan; what he earns goes to his own matriarchal stock, and at his death his bones are deposited in the cromlech of his mother's kin.

Such testimony cannot be put aside. I wish it were possible for me to give a detailed account of this people, there is so much that is of interest to us in their mother-right customs. All that I can do is to note briefly a few of these, which to me seem specially important.

And first, in order to understand better their customs, let us consider a few facts of the people themselves. The Khasis are a vigorous and sturdy race. The men are short, but exceedingly muscular; the women are comely, especially when young; and the children are remarkably pretty. In both the sexes strongly developed calves are considered a mark of beauty. It is interesting to note that the men usually wear their hair long, and when it is cut short, a single lock is preserved at the back, which is called *u niuhtrong*, "the grandmother's lock." In some districts the men pull out the hairs of the moustaches, with the exception of a few hairs on either side of the upper lip. In character these people are independent, simple, truthful and straightforward; cheerful in disposition, and light-hearted by nature. They thoroughly appreciate a joke, especially the women. Among the men there is some drunkenness, but not among the women, though they are the chief distillers of spirits. Men and women work together, usually at the same occupations. We learn that the Khasis have an unusual love of nature, and are fond of music; thus they have names for birds and flowers, also for many butterflies and moths. These are traits not usually found in the people of India.

There is a point to note of special interest in their language. All the nouns have a masculine and a feminine gender, and the feminine nouns immensely predominate. The sun is feminine, the moon masculine. In the pronouns there is one form only in the plural, and that is feminine. It may seem that these matters — noted so briefly — are unimportant; but it is such little things that deserve attentive study. At least they serve to show that the Khasis have reached a high level of primitive culture; and they indicate further the strong importance of the feminine idea, which is the main interest in our inquiry.

A few words must be said about the organisation of the tribes. These tribes are formed in sections — of which the chief are the Khasi, Synteng, and War. Each section or tribe is divided into clans and sub-clans; these are strictly exogamous. To marry within the clan is the greatest sin a Khasi can commit. This would explain the strict reckoning of descent through the mothers.

The Khasi clan grew from the family. There is a saying common among the people, *Long jaid ne ka kynthei,* "From the woman sprang the tribe." All the clans trace their descent from ancestresses (grandmothers) who are called *Ki Iwabei Tynrai,* literally, *grandmothers of the root,* i. e. *the root of the tree of the clan.* In some clans the name of the ancestress survives, as, for instance, *Kyngas houning,* "the sweet one." *Ka Iaw shubde* is the ancestress of the Synteng tribe, and it is curious to note that she is credited with having first introduced the art of smelting iron. She is also said to have founded a market in which she successfully traded in cattle.[74]

It is hardly possible to exaggerate the esteem in which the tribal ancestress is held; she is so greatly reverenced that she may truly be said to be deified. In such worship rests the foundation of the deep tribal piety. *Ka Iawbei,* "the first mother," has the foremost place of honour by her side, and acting as her agent is *U Suid Nia,* her brother. There is another fact to show the honour in which the female ideal is held. The flat memorial stones set up to perpetuate the memory of the dead are called after the mothers of the clan, while the standing stones ranged behind them are dedicated to the male kinsmen on the female side. These table stones are exceedingly interesting. They are exactly like the long stones and dolmens which are found in

Brittany, in Ireland, in Galicia in Spain, and other parts of Europe. Is it possible that some of these memorials, whose history has been lost, were also set up to commemorate the mothers of tribes? But be this as it may, among the Khasis, where ancient custom and tradition have been preserved, goddesses are more important than gods. Almost all the other deities to whom propitiation is offered are female. Male personages also figure, and among them *Thaulang*, the husband, is revered.[75] Still the chief divinity rests in the goddesses; the gods are represented only in their relation to them. The powers of sickness and death are all female, and these are most frequently worshipped. Again, the protectors of the household are goddesses. I wish that I had space to write of their curious, yet beautiful, religious rites. The sacrifices are communal in character; they are offered in times of sickness and when dangers threaten the clan. Priestesses assist at all sacrifices and the male officiants act only as their agents. The household sacrifices are always performed by women.

Consider what this placing of their goddesses rather than their gods — of the priestess rather than priest — in the forefront of their worship signifies! Very plainly it reflects honour on the sex to which the supreme deities belong. We need no clearer proof of the high status of women among this people. Such customs are certainly survivals[76] from the time of a more primitive matriarchate, when the priestess was the agent for the performance of all religious ceremonies. In one state a priestess still performs the sacrifices on the appointment of a new Siem, or ruler. Another such survival is the High Priestess of Nongkrem, in the Synteng district, who "combines in her person sacerdotal and regal functions." In this state the tradition runs that the first High Priestess was *Ka Pah Synten*, "the flower-lured one." She was a beautiful maiden, who had her abode in a cave at Marai, near Nongkrem whence she was enticed by means of a flower. She was taken by her lover to be his bride, and she became not only the first High Priestess of Nongkrem, but also the mother of the Siems of Nongkrem.

It must be noted that the Siems or rulers of the states are always men. They are chosen from the eldest sister's children. Possibly the case of the High Priestess of Nongkrem, who is the nominal head of the state, points to an earlier period of rule by women; but today the temporal power is delegated to one of her sons or nephews, who becomes the Siem. I need not labour this question overmuch; it is actualities I wish to deal with. As I have repeatedly said, there is no sure ground for believing that the maternal system involves rule by women. This may have happened in some cases, but I do not think that it can ever have been common. I am very certain, however, of the error in the view which accepts the subordination of women as the common condition among barbarous peoples, whereas there are indications and proofs in all directions of a more or less strong assertiveness on their part, and always in the direction of social unity and sexual regulation. The fact that the maternal system resulted in the limitation of the freedom of the male members of the family is, in my opinion, to be attributed to those powerful female qualities which exercised an immense influence on early societies. Regarding what has been said, I think it cannot be denied that while individual rights were of far more importance to the males, the idea of the family and social rights were, in their turn, essentially feminine sentiments. Thus it was in the women's interest to consolidate the family, and by means of this their own power; and they succeeded in doing so to an extraordinary extent in primitive communities, without help of the maternal customs, which, as I have tried to make clear, arose out of the conditions of the primordial family and by the action of the united mothers. If I am right, then, here is the primary cause of the women's position of authority in the communal maternal family.

I am very certain of the rights such a system conferred upon women; rights that are impossible under the patriarchal family, which involves the subordination of the woman to her father first and afterward to her husband. In proof of this let us now consider marriage and divorce, the laws of inheritance, and other customs of the Khasis. And first we may note that polygamy — the distinctive custom of the patriarchs — does not exist; as Mr Gurdon remarks, "such a practice would not be in vogue among a people who observe the matriarchate." This is the more remarkable as the Khasi women considerably outnumber the men. In 1901 there were 1118 females to 1000 males. At the present time the people are monandrists. There are instances of men having wives other than those they regularly marry, but the practice is not common. Such wives are called "stolen wives," and their children are said "to be from the top," *i. e.* from the branches of the clan and not the root. In the War country the children of the "stolen wife" enjoy an equal share in the father's property with the children of the regular wife. Polyandry is said to be practised, but the fact is not mentioned by Mr Gurdon; in any case it can prevail only among the poorer sort, with whom, too, it would often seem to mean rather facility of divorce than the simultaneous admission of plurality of husbands.[77]

The courtship customs of Khasi youths and maidens are simple and beautiful. The young people meet at the dances in the springtime, when the girls choose their future husbands. There is no practice among the Khasis of exchange of daughters; and there is an entire absence of the patriarchal idea of their women as property. Marriage is a simple contract, unaccompanied by any ceremony.[78] After marriage the husband lives with his wife in her mother's home. Of late years a new custom has arisen, and now in the Khasi tribe, when one or two children have been born, and *if the marriage is a happy one,* the couple frequently leave the family home, and set up housekeeping for themselves. When this is done, husband and wife pool their earnings for the support of the family. This is clearly a departure from the maternal marriage, a step in the direction of father-right. Among the Syntengs, the people who have most closely preserved the customs of the matriarchate, the husband does not even go to live with his wife, he only visits her in her mother's home. In Joway this rule is so strict that the husband comes only after dark. He is not permitted to sleep, to eat, or smoke during his visit — the idea being that as none of his earnings go to support the home, he must not partake of food or any refreshment. Here is a curious instance of etiquette preserving these clandestine visits long after the time when such secrecy was necessary. We may note another survival among the Syntengs. The father is commonly called by the name of the first child, thus, the father of a child called Bobon, becomes Pa-bobon.[79] This does not, I am sure, point back to a period when paternity was uncertain, rather, it is an effort to establish the social relation of the father to the family, and is connected with domestic and property considerations, not at all with relationship. The proof of this will appear in a later chapter.

Very striking are the conditions attaching to divorce. Again we find the right of separation granted equally to both sexes, a significant indication of the high position of women. Marriage being regarded as an agreement between wife and husband, the tie may be broken without any question of disgrace. But although divorce is frequent and easy, and can be claimed for a variety of reasons, all who have dwelt among the Khasis testify to the durable and happy marriages among them. Only when they find it impossible to live amicably together do a couple agree to separate. In this event the children always remain with the mother. For their mothers the children cherish a very strong affection, for all their sympathies and affection bind them to her and her family.

The conditions of divorce vary in the separate tribes. Among the Khasis both parties must agree to the dissolution of the tie. With the Synteng and War tribes such mutual consent is not necessary, but the partner who claims release from the other, without his or her consent, must pay compensation. A woman cannot be divorced during pregnancy. The form of divorce is simple; among the Khasis it consists of the exchange of five cowries. This is done in the presence of witnesses, and the ceremony must take place in the open air. Then a crier goes around the village to proclaim the divorce, using the following words:

> *Kaw*—hear, oh villagers! that—U and K have been separated in the presence of the elders. *Hei!* thou, oh young men, canst go

and make love to K — for she is now unmarried, and thou, oh maidens, canst make love to U — *Hei!* there is no let or hindrance from henceforth.

And here I would pause, although it leads me a little aside, to make a point that to me seems to be of special importance. Obviously this simple divorce by mutual consent was made easy in its working by the maternal system. The great drawback to the dissolution of the marriage tie in the patriarchal family is the effect it has on the lives of the children; but in the maternal family such evil does not exist, for the children always live with the mother and take her name. By saying this, I do not wish to imply that I am necessarily recommending such a system, but that it had its advantages for the mother and her children, I think, cannot be denied. Its failure arises, as is evident, from the alien position of the father in relation to his children.

In the primitive maternal family the place of the father, to a great extent, is filled by the maternal uncle. Among the Khasis he is regarded in the light of a father. It is his duty to assist the mother in the management of the family. The husband is looked upon merely as *u shong kha,*[80] a begetter. Only by the later marriage custom, when the wife and children leave the home of her mother, has the father any recognised position in the home. "There is no gainsaying the fact," writes Mr Gurdon, "that the husband is a stranger in the wife's home, and it is certain he can take no part in the rites and ceremonies of his wife's family."

The important status assigned to women becomes clearer when we consider the laws of inheritance. Daughters inherit, not sons. The youngest daughter is heiress to the family property, but the other daughters are entitled to a share on the mother's death. No man can possess property unless it is self-acquired. Among the Synteng, such property on the man's death goes to his mother. This would seem to be the primitive custom. There is now a provision that, if the wife undertakes not to remarry she has half of her husband's property, which descends to her youngest daughter. In the Khasi states a man's property, if acquired before his marriage, goes to his mother, but what is gained afterwards goes to the wife, for the youngest daughter. Only in the War country do the sons inherit from the father with the daughters, but something in addition is given to the youngest daughter. The family property always descends in the female line. For this reason, daughters are of more importance than sons. A family without daughters dies out, which among the Khasis is the greatest calamity, as there is no one qualified to bury the dead and perform the religious rites. Thus both the Khasis and the Syntengs have a plan of adoption. The male members of any family, if left without females, are allowed to call in a young girl from another family to perform the family religious ceremonies. She takes the place of the youngest daughter, and becomes the head of the household. She inherits the ancestral property.

In the face of these facts it can hardly be denied that mother-right and mother-power among the Khasis are still very much alive. Here at least descent through the mother does involve power to women, and confers exceptional rights, especially as regards inheritance. I have already called attention to the equality of the women with men in the code of sexual morality. This is so important that it is worth while to follow it a little further. That freedom in love carries with it domestic and social rights and privileges to women I have no longer to prove. We found the same freedom under the maternal family among the Iroquois and Zuñi Indians: there courtship was in the hands of the woman; there also divorce was free, and a couple would rather separate than live together inharmoniously. I have given proof of the happy domestic life of these peoples. Equality in the sexual relationships has always been closely associated with the status of women. Wherever divorce is difficult, there woman's lot is hard, and her position low. It is part of the patriarchal custom which regards the man as the owner of the woman. It would be easy to prove this by the history of marriage in the races of the past, as also by an examination of the present divorce laws in civilised countries. I cannot do this, but I make the assertion without the least shadow of doubt. "Free divorce is the charter of

Woman's Freedom." I would point back in proof to these examples of the maternal family, foremost among whose privileges is this equality of partnership in marriage. Here you have before you, solved by these primitive peoples, some of the most urgent questions that yet have to be faced by us today. To hear of peoples who live gladly, and without those problems that are rotting away our civilisation, brings a new courage to those of us, who sometimes grow hopeless at our own needless wastage of love and life.

I must not say more upon this question, though it is one that tempts me strongly. It is not, however, my purpose in this book to offer opinions of my own on these problems of the relations of the two sexes; I prefer to leave the facts of the mother-age to speak for themselves. Those whose eyes are not blinded will not fail to see.[81]

Further Examples of the Maternal Family

PURSUING OUR INQUIRY into the social organisation of mother-right, an interesting example occurs among the peoples of the Malay States, where, notwithstanding the centres of Hindu and Moslem influence, much has been retained of the maternal system, once universally prevalent. The maternal marriage, here known as the *ambel-anak*, in which the husband lives with the wife, paying nothing to the support of the family and occupying a subordinate position, may be taken as typical of the former condition. But among the tribes who have come in contact with outside influences the custom of the husband visiting the wife, or residing in her house, is modified, and in some cases has altogether disappeared.

From a private correspondent, a resident in the Malay States, I have received some interesting notes about the present conditions of the native tribes and the position of women. "In most of the Malay States exogamous matriarchy has in comparatively modern times been superseded by feudalism (*i. e.*, the patriarchal rights of the father). But where the old customs survive, the women are still to a large extent in control. The husband goes to live in the wife's village; thus the women in each group are a compact unity, while the men are strangers to each other and enter as unorganised individuals. This is the real basis of the women's power. In other tribes, where the old customs have changed, the women occupy a distinctly inferior position, and under the influence of Islam the idea of secluding adult women has been for centuries spreading and increasing in force." Here, again, clear proof is shown of the maternal system exercising a direct influence on the position of women. And this statement is in agreement with Robertson Smith, who, in writing of the maternal marriage, says: "And it is remarkable that when both customs — the woman receiving her husband in her own hut, and the man taking his wife to his — occur side by side among the same people, descent in the former case is traced through the mother, in the latter through the father."[82]

In its ancient form the maternal communal family has notably persisted among the Padang Highlanders of Sumatra. These people live in village communities, with long timber houses placed in barrack-like rows, very similar to the communal dwellings of the American Indians. The houses are gay in appearance, and are adorned with carved and coloured woodwork. One dwelling will contain as many as a hundred people, who form a *sa-mandei,* or mother-hood. Again we find the family consisting of the house-mother and her descendants in the female line — sons and daughters, and the daughters' children. McGee thus describes these maternal households:[83]

> If the visitor, mounting the ladder steps, looks in at one of the doors of the separate dwellings, he may see seated beyond the family hearth the mother and her children, eating the midday meal, and very likely the father, who may have been doing a turn of work in his wife's rice-plot. If he is a kindly husband, he is there much as a friendly visitor, but his real home remains in the house in which he was born.

The husband has no permanent residence in the woman's house, and at dusk each evening the men may be seen walking across the village to join their wives and families. The father has no rights over his children, who belong wholly to the wife's *suku,* or clan. But this in no way implies that the father is unknown, for monogamy is the rule; as is usual the question is one rather of social right than of relationship. The maternal uncle is the male head of the house, and exercises under the mother the duties of a father to the children. The brother of the eldest grandmother is the male head of the family settlement and the clan consists of a number of these families. It would seem that these male rulers act as the agents of the female members, whose authority is great. This power is dependent on the inheritance; as is the descent, so is the property, and its transmission is arranged for the benefit of the maternal lineage. For this reason daughters are preferred rather than sons.

This account of the Padang Malays may be supplemented by the Jesuit missionary De Mailla's description of the maternal marriage in the Island of Formosa.[84] Speaking of this marriage, McGee says: "If it had received the notice it deserves, it might long ago have placed the study of maternal institutions on a sounder basis."

> The Formosan youth wishing to marry makes music day by day at the maid's door, till, if willing, she comes out to him, and when they are agreed, the parents are told, and the marriage feast is prepared in the bride's house, whence the bridegroom returns no more to his father, regarding his father-in-law's house as his own, and himself as the support of it, while his own father's house is no more to him than in Europe the bride's home is henceforth to her when she quits it to live with her husband. Thus the Formosans set no store on sons, but aspire to have daughters, who procure them sons-in-law to become the support of their old age.

It will be noted that here the house is spoken of as the father's, and not as belonging to the mother. The bridegroom is the suitor, and we see the creeping in of property considerations always associated with the rise of father-right. Though the husband has as yet no recognised position and lives in the wife's home, he is valued for his service to his father-in-law, clearly a step in the direction of property assertion. Among many of the Malay hill tribes of Formosa the maternal system is dying out, though the old law forbidding marriage within the clan remains in force.

These changes must be expected wherever the transition towards father-right has begun; the older forms of courtship and marriage, so favourable to the woman, are replaced by patriarchal customs. One or two curious examples of primitive courtship, in which the initiative is taken entirely by the girl may be noted here. Among the Garos tribe it is not only the privilege, but the duty of the girl to select her lover, while an infringement of this rule is severely and summarily punished. Any declaration made on the part of the young man is regarded as an insult to the whole *mahári* (motherhood) to which the girl belongs, a stain only to be expiated by liberal presents made at the expense of the *mahári* of the over-forward lover. The marriage customs are equally curious. On the morning of the wedding a ceremony very similar to capture takes place, only it is the bridegroom who is abducted. He pretends to be unwilling and runs away and hides, but he is caught by the friends of the bride. Then he is taken by force, weeping as he goes, in spite of the resistance and counterfeited grief of his parents and friends, to the bride's house, where he takes up his residence with his mother-in-law. It is instructive to find that these marriages are usually successful. Although divorce is easy, it is not frequent. "The Garos will not hastily make engagements, because, when they do make them, they intend to keep them."[85]

In Paraguay, we are told, the women are generally endowed with stronger passions than the men, and are allowed to make the proposals.[86] So also among the Ahitas of the Philippine Islands, where, if her clan-parents will not consent to a love match the girl seizes the young man by the hair, carries him off, and declares she has run away with him. In such a case it appears the marriage is held to be valid whether the parents consent or not.[87] A similar custom of a gentler character, is practised by the Tarrahumari Indians of Northern Mexico, among whom, according to Lumboltz, the maiden is a persistent wooer employing a *répertoire* of really exquisite love songs to soften the heart of a reluctant swain.[88] Again, in New

Guinea, where the women held a very independent position, "the girl is always regarded as the seducer. Women steal men." A youth who proposed to a girl would be making himself ridiculous, would be called a woman, and laughed at by the girls. The usual method by which a girl proposes is to send a present to the youth by a third party, following this up by repeated gifts of food; the young man sometimes waits a month or two, receiving presents all the time, in order to assure himself of the girl's constancy, before decisively accepting her advances.[89]

It is clear that these cases, which I have chosen from a number of similar courtship customs, differ very much from what is our idea of the customary role of the girl and her lover. To me they are very instructive. They show the error of the long-held belief in the passivity of the female as a natural law of the sex.[90] Such openness of conduct in courtship is impossible except where women hold an entirely independent position. Here, then, is another advantage that may be claimed as arising for women out of the maternal system. I claim this: the woman's right of selection in love — yes, her greatest right, one that is necessary for a freer and more beautiful mating.

Terminating this short digression, I return to my examination of the peoples among whom the family is especially maternal.

The Pelew Islanders of the South Sea have customs in many respects the same as those of the Khasi tribes. They preserve strict maternal descent, and like the Khasis, the deities of all the clans are goddesses. The life and social habits of the people have been described by Kubary, a careful and sympathetic observer, for long resident in the island.[91] The tribes are divided into exogamous clans, and intermarriage between any relations on the mother's side is unlawful. These clans are grouped together in villages and the life is of a communal character. Each village consists of about a score of clans, and forms with its lands a petty independent state.

Again we find the maternal system intimately connected with religious ideas, and it is interesting to recall what was said by Bachofen: "Wherever gynaecocracy meets us the mystery of religion is bound up with it, and lends to motherhood an incorporation in some divinity." Among these Islanders every family traces its descent from a woman — the common mother of the clan. And for this reason the members worship a goddess and not a god. In the different states there are, besides other special deities, usually a goddess and a god, but as these are held to be derived directly from a household-goddess, it is evident that here, as among the Khasis, goddesses are older than the gods. This is shown also by the names of the goddesses. There is another fact of interest: some women are reputed to be the wives of the gods, they are called *Amalalieys* and have a great honour paid to them, while their children pass for the offspring of the gods.

The reverence paid to the ancestral goddesses is explained by Mr Kubary as arising from the importance of women in the clans.

> "The existence of the clan depends entirely on the life of the women, and not at all on the life of the men. If the women survive, it is no matter though every man in the clan should perish, for the women will, as usual, marry men of another clan, and their offspring will inherit their mother's clan, and thereby prolong its existence. Whereas if the women of the clan die out the clan necessarily becomes extinct, even if every man in it should survive; for the men must, as usual, marry women of another clan, and their offspring will inherit their mother's clan and not the clan of the father, which accordingly, with the death of the father, is wiped off the community.

I quote this passage because it shows so clearly what I am claiming, that descent through the mother, under the condition of strict exogamy, conferred a very marked distinction on the female members of the clan, whose existence depended on them; this cannot possibly have failed to act favourably on their position. I may note, too, in passing, the fallacy of Mr McLennan's view that polyandry (which, it will be remembered, he held to have been developed from and connected with mother-descent) arose as a result of female infanticide. Such a practice is clearly impossible in clans whose existence depends on the life of its female members; daughters among them are prised more highly than sons.

The case we are now examining affords the strongest confirmation of the honour paid to women under the strict maternal system. Take alone the titles that these Pelew islanders give to their women, as *Adhalál a pelú*, "mothers of the land," and *Adhalál a blay*, "mothers of the clan." The testimony of those who know their customs is that the women enjoy complete equality with the men in every respect. Mr Kubary affirms the predominance of female influence in all the social life of the clan. He asserts, without qualification, that the women both politically and socially enjoy a position superior to that of the men. The eldest women in the clans exercise the most decisive influence in the conduct of affairs; the head men do nothing without full consultation with them, and their power extends to affairs of state and even to foreign politics. No chief would venture to come to a decision without the approval of the mothers of the families. As one consequence of this power the women have clubs of association similar to the clubs of men that are common in so many tribes. A curious privilege given to women is recorded: "The women have an unlimited privilege of striking, fining, or if it be done on the spot, killing any man who makes his way into their bathing places."[92]

The marriage customs I shall pass over briefly, as they are similar to those of other tribes under the maternal system, though changes may be noted, such, for instance, as presents in the form of a kind of bride-price being given by the bridegroom to the parents of the bride. This is not a maternal custom, and although half of such presents belongs by right to the girl, it is clearly a form of wife-purchase. Then polygamy is practised, though it is expressly stated to be uncommon.[93] There is now a marriage ceremony. Divorce still remains free, and the conditions are favourable for the wife. Jealousy is said to be prevalent both among the men and the women. The wedding monologue is interesting and indicates the relative position of the female and male members of the family. The salutation is as follows:

> Hei, thou, oh mother; oh grandmothers; oh maternal uncle; oh elder grandmother; oh younger grandfather; oh elder grandfather! As the flesh has fallen the ring has been put on.... You will all of you give ear [the ancestresses and ancestors] you will continue giving strength and spirit that they [the bride and bridegroom] may be well.

There is left an important fact to consider, which explains the persistence of the women's authority under marriage conditions much less favourable than the complete maternal form. The Pelew women have another source of power; their position has an industrial as well as a kinship basis. In this island the people subsist mainly on the produce of their taro fields, and the cultivation of this, their staple food, is carried out by the women alone. And this identification of women with the industrial process has without doubt contributed materially to the predominance of female influence on the social life of the people. Wherever the control over the means of production is in the hands of women, we find them exercising influence and even authority. Among these islanders the women do not merely bestow life on the people, they also work to obtain that which is most essential for the preservation of life, and therefore they are called "mothers of the land."[94] Now, considering this honour paid to the Pelew women, it is clearly impossible to regard their work in cultivating the taro as a sign of their subordinate position in the social order. The facts of primitive life are often mistaken. This is a question to which I shall refer again in a later chapter.

In the same way among the Pani Kotches, tribes of Bengal, we find the women in a privileged position, due to their greater industrial activity and intelligence.

"It is the women's business to dig the soil, to sow and plant, as well as to spin, weave and brew beer; they refuse no task, and leave only the coarsest labour to the men. The mother of the family marries her daughter at an early age; at the feast of betrothal she dispenses half as much again to the bride as to the bridegroom-elect. As for the grown-up girls and the widows, they know very well how to find husbands; the wealthy never lack partners. The chosen one goes to reside with his mother-in-law, who both reigns and governs, with her daughter for prime minister. If the consort permits himself to incur expenses without special authorisation, he must meet them as best he can. Fathers of families have been known to be sold as slaves, the wives refusing to pay the penalties they incurred. Under these circumstances, it was lawful for them to marry again."[95]

Here, as among the Pelew islanders, special industrial conditions are combined with the maternal system, and as a result we find what may, perhaps, be termed "an economic matriarchy." Another cause of authority, quite as powerful, is the possession by women of inherited property. Among barbarous peoples the importance of this is not so great, but where mother-descent has, for any reason, been maintained up to a time when individual possession has been developed and property is large, we meet with a remarkable "pecuniary matriarchate," based on the women holding the magic power of money.

An example may be found in the interesting Touaregs of the Sahara, a race very far advanced in civilisation, who, even at the present day, have preserved their independence and many of their ancient customs. Among them all relationship is still maternal and confers both rank and inheritance. "The child follows the blood of the mother," and the son of a slave or serf father and a noble woman is noble. "It is the womb which dyes the child," the Touaregs say in their primitive language.[96] All property descends only through the mother, and by means of accumulation the greatest part of the fortune of the community is in the hands of women. This is the real basis of the women's power. "Absolute mistress of her fortune, her actions, and her children, who belong to her and bear her name, the Targui woman goes where she will and exercises a real authority." The unusual position of the wife is significantly indicated by the fact that, although polygamy is permitted by the law, she practically enforces monogamy, for the conditions of divorce are so favourable for a woman that she can at once separate from a husband who attempts to give her a rival. Again the initiative in courtship is taken by the woman, who chooses from her suitors the one whom she herself prefers.[97]

It is interesting to note that the Targui women know how to read and write in greater numbers than the men. Duveyrier states that to them is due the preservation of the ancient Libyan and Berber writings.[98] "Leaving domestic work to their slaves, the Targui ladies occupy themselves with reading, writing, music and embroidery; they live as intelligent aristocrats."[99] "The ladies of the tribe of Ifoghas, in particular, are renowned for their *savoirvivre* and their musical talent; they know how to ride *mehari* better than all their rivals. Secure in their cages, they can ride races with the most intrepid cavaliers, if one may give this name to riders on dromedaries; in order, also, to keep themselves in practice in this kind of riding, they meet to take short trips together, going wherever they like without the escort of any man."[100] In the tribe of Imanan, who are descended from the ancient sultans, the women are given the title *Timanôkalîn*, "royal women," on account of their beauty and their talent in the art of music. They often give concerts, to which the men come "from long distances — decked out like male ostriches." In these concerts the women improvise the songs, accompanying themselves on the tambourine and a sort of violin or *rebâza*. They are much sought after in marriage, because of the title of *cherif* which they confer on their children.[101]

There is a touch of chivalrous sentiment in the relations between men and women.[102] "If a woman is married," Duveyrier tells us, "she is honoured all the more in proportion to the number of her masculine friends, but she must not show preference to any one of them. The lady may embroider on the cloak, or write on the shield of her chevalier, verses in his praise and wishes for his good fortune. Her friend may, without being censured, cut the name of the lady on the rocks or chant her virtues. 'Friends of different sexes,' say the

Touaregs, 'are for the eyes and heart, and not for the bed only, as among the Arabs.'"[103] Letourneau, in quoting these passages from Duveyrier, makes the following comment: "Such customs as these indicate delicate instincts, which are absolutely foreign to the Arabs. They strongly remind us of the times of our southern troubadours and of the *cours d'amour,* which were the quintessence of chivalry."[104]

The foregoing example is exceedingly interesting; it shows women holding the position that as a rule belongs to men, and is thus worthy of most careful study, but at the same time we must guard against according it a general value which it does not possess. Such a case is exceptional, though it by no means stands alone, and the social position of Targui women is analogous to that of the women of ancient Egypt. It is important to note that their great independence arose through the persistence of maternal descent, and could not have been maintained apart from that system, which placed in their hands the strong power of wealth. Here, then, is certain proof of the favourable influence mother-descent may exercise on the status of women. It is because of this I have brought forward this example of the Targui women.

Enough has now been said. I have examined the institution of the maternal family, both in the early communal stage and also under later social conditions, where, in certain cases, mother-descent has been maintained. In all the examples cited I have given the marriage customs and domestic habits of the people as they are testified to by authorities whose records cannot be questioned. Many similar examples, it may be said, might be brought forward from other races, and the proof of mother-right and mother-power greatly strengthened thereby. There is, however, so much similarity in the maternal family, so much correspondence in the marriage forms and social habits prevailing among races widely separated, that the points of difference are little in comparison with those they have in common. My object is not so much to exhaust the subject as to bring into relief the radical differences between the maternal communal clan, with its social life centred around the mothers, and the opposite patriarchal form in which the solitary family is founded on the individual father. I hold that, other conditions being equal, the one system is favourable to the authority of women, the other to the authority of men. The facts which have been cited are, I submit, amply sufficient to support this view.

We have seen that the life of the maternal clan is dependent on the women — and not upon the men; we have noted that the inheritance of the family name and the family property passing through the women adds considerably to their importance, and that daughters are preferred to sons. We have found women the organisers of the households, the guardians of the household stores, and the distributors of food, under a social organisation that may be termed "a communal matriarchy." More important than all else, we have noted the remarkable freedom of women in the sexual relationships; in courtship they are permitted to take the active part; in marriage their position is one of such power that, sometimes, they are able to impose the form of the marriage; in divorce they enjoy equal, and even superior, rights of separation; moreover, they are always the owners and controllers of the children. Nor is the influence of women restricted to the domestic sphere. We have found them the advisers, and in some cases the dictators, in the social organisation under the headmen of the clan. Then we examined the cases in which the women's power has an industrial as well as a kinship basis, and have proved the existence of an "economic matriarchy." And further even than this, we have found women the sole possessors of accumulated wealth, and noted that, under the favourable conditions of such a "pecuniary matriarchy," they are able to obtain a position in learning and the arts excelling that of the men. We have even seen goddesses set above the gods, and women worshipped as deities.

Now I submit to the judgment of my readers — what do these examples of mother-right show, if not that, broadly speaking, women were the dominant force in this stage of the family. No doubt too much importance may be attached to the idea of women ruling. This is an error I have tried to guard against. My aim throughout has been to establish mother-right, not mother-rule. I believe it is only by an extraordinary power of illusion that we can recognise, in the favourable position of women under mother-descent Bachofen's view of an Amazonian gynaecocracy. But this does not weaken at all my position. I maintain that such customs of courtship, marriage and divorce, of property inheritance and possession, and of the domestic and social rights, as those we have seen in the cases examined, afford conclusive proof of women's power in the maternal family. If this is denied, the only conclusion that suggests itself to me is that, those who seek to diminish the power of mother-right have done so in reinforcement of a preconceived idea of the superiority of the man as the natural and unchanging order in the relationships of the sexes. One suspects prejudice here. To approach this question with any fairness, it is absolutely essential to clear the mind from the current theories regarding the family. The order is not sacred in the sense that it has always had the same form. It is this belief in the immutability of our form of marriage and the family which accounts for the prejudice with which this question is approached. The modern civilised man cannot easily accustom himself to the idea that in the maternal family the dominion of the mother was regarded as the natural, and, therefore, the right and accepted order of the family. It is very difficult for us even to believe in a relationship of the mother and the father that is so exactly opposite to that with which we are accustomed.

Mother-Right Customs and the Transition to Father-Right

ENDEAVOUR HAS BEEN made in the previous chapters to present the case for mother-right as clearly and concisely as possible. The point we have now reached is this: while mother-right does not constitute or make necessary rule by women, under that system they enjoy considerable power as the result (1) of their organised position under the maternal marriage among their own clan-kindred, (2) of their importance to the male members of the clan as the transmitters and holders of property.

It is necessary to remember the close connection between these mother-right customs and the communal clan, which was a free association for mutual protection. This is a point of much interest. As we have seen, the undivided family of the clan could be maintained only by descent through the mothers, since its existence depended on its power to retain and protect all its members. In this way it destroyed the solitary family, by its opposition to the authority and will of the husband and father.

These conclusions will be strengthened as we continue our examination of mother-right customs as we shall find them in all parts of the world. I must select a few examples only and describe them very briefly, not because these cases offer less interest than the complete maternal families already examined, but because of the length to which this part of my inquiry is rapidly growing. The essential fact to establish is the prevalence of mother-descent as a probable universal stage in the past history of mankind, and then to show the causes which, by undermining the dominion of the maternal clan, led to the adoption of father-right and the re-establishment of the patriarchal family.

Let us begin with Australia, where the aboriginal population is in a more primitive condition than any other race whose institutions have been investigated. I can notice a few facts only from the harvest of information brought together by anthropologists and travellers. The tribes are grouped into exogamous sub-divisions, and each group has its own land from which it takes a local name. Each group wanders about on its own territory in order to hunt game and collect roots, sometimes in detached families and, less often, in larger hordes, for there seems to be a tendency to local isolation. A remarkable feature of the social organisation is found in the more advanced tribes, where, in addition to the division into clans, the group is divided into male and female classes. All the members of such clans regard themselves as kinsmen, or brothers and sisters; they have the same totem mark and are bound to protect each other. The totem bond is stronger than any blood tie, while the sex totems are even more sacred than the clan totems.

Much confusion has arisen out of the attempts to explain the Australian system; and for long the close totem kinship was supposed to afford evidence of group marriage, by which a man of one clan was held to have sexual rights over all the women in another clan. But further insight into their customs has proved the error of such a view, which arose from a misunderstanding of the terms of relationship used among the tribes. Nowhere is marriage bound by more severe laws; death is the penalty for sexual intercourse with a person of a forbidden clan. And it is certain that there is no evidence at all of communism in wives.[105]

A system of taboos is very strongly established, and as we should expect the women appear to be most active in maintaining these sexual separations. If a man, even by mistake, kills the sex-totem of the women, they are as much enraged as if it were one of their own children, and they will turn and attack him with their long poles.

In Australia it is easy to recognise a very early stage in human society. The organisation of the family group into the clan is still taking place. Moreover, the most primitive patriarchal conditions have not greatly changed, for the males are great individualists and cannot readily suffer the rights of others than themselves. Mother-right can hardly be said to exist, and the position of women is low. It is not the custom among any tribes for the husband to reside in the home of the wife; this in itself is sufficient to explain the power of the husbands. Wives are frequently obtained by capture, and fights for women are of common occurrence. Here it would seem that progress has been very slow. Indeed, it is the chief interest of the Australian tribes that we can trace the transformation from the early patriarchal conditions to the communal clan.

There is still another fact of very special interest. In the large majority of tribes known to us descent is traced through the mother; the proportion of these tribes to those with father-descent being four to one. Now, the question arises as to which of these two systems is the earlier custom? As a rule it is assumed that in all cases descent was originally traced through the mother. But is this really so? The evidence of the Australian tribes points to the exact opposite opinion. For what do we find? The tribes that have established mother-descent have advanced further, with a more developed social organisation, which could hardly be the case if they were the more primitive. To this question Starcke, in *The Primitive Family*, has drawn particular attention; he regards "the female line as a later development," arrived at after descent through the father was recognised, such change being due to an urgent necessity which arose in the primitive family for cohesion among its members, making necessary sexual regulation and the maternal clan.

It is certainly difficult to decide on the priority of this or that custom. But what is significant is that in Australia the tribes which maintain the male line of descent must be assigned to the lowest stage of development. The rights established by marriage among them are less clearly defined, and the use of the totem marks, with the sexual taboos arising from them, are less developed. Everything tends to show that clan organisation and union in peace have arisen with mother-descent, which cannot thus be regarded as a survival from the earlier order, but as a later development — a step forward in progress and social regulation.

I take this as being exceedingly important: it serves to establish what it has been my purpose to show, that in the first stage the family was patriarchal — small hostile groups living under the jealous authority of the fathers; and that only as advancement came did the maternal clan develop, since it arose through a community of purpose binding all its members in peace, and thereby controlling the warring individual interests. The reasons for mother-descent have been altogether misunderstood by those who regard it as the earliest phase of the family, and connect the custom with sexual disorder and uncertainty of paternity. In all cases the clan system shows a marked organisation, with a much stronger cohesion than is possible in the restricted family, which is held together by the force of the father. It was within the clan that the rights of the father and husband were endangered: he lost his position as supreme head of the family, and became an alien member in a free association where his position was strictly defined. The incorporation of the family into the clan arose through the struggle for existence forcing it into association; it was the subordinate position of the husband under such a system which finally made the women the rulers of the household. If we regard the social conditions of the maternal system as the first stage of development, they are as difficult to understand as they become intelligible when we consider it as a later and beneficent phase in the growth of society.

This, then, I claim as the chief good of the maternal system. As I see it, each advance in progress rests on the conquest of sexual distrusts and fierceness forcing into isolation. These jealous and odious monopolist instincts have been the bane of humanity. Each race must inevitably in the end outlive them; they are the surviving relics of the ape and the tiger. They arise out of that self-concentration and intensity of animalism that binds the hands of men and women from taking their inheritance. The brute in us still resents association. Am I wrong in connecting this individual monopolist idea of My power! My right! with the paternal as opposed to the maternal family? At any rate I find it absent in the communal clan grouped around the mothers, where the enlarged family makes common cause and life is lived by all for and with each other.

An instructive example of the joint maternal family is furnished by the Nairs of Malabar, where we see a very late development of the clan system. The family group includes many allied families, who live together in large communal houses and possess everything in common. There is common tenure of land, over which the eldest male member of the community presides; while the mother, and after her death the eldest daughter, is the ruler in the household. It is impossible to give the details of their curious conjugal customs. The men do not marry, but frequent other houses as lovers, without ceasing to live at home, and without being in any way detached from the maternal family. There is, however, a symbolic marriage for every girl, by a rite known as tying the *tali*; but this marriage serves the purpose only of initiation, and the couple separate after one day. When thus prepared for marriage, a Nair girl chooses her lovers, and any number of unions may be entered upon without any restrictions other than the strict prohibitions relative to caste and tribe. These later marriages, unlike the solemn initial rite, have no ceremony connected with them, and are entered into freely at the will of the woman and her family.[106]

Now, if we regard these customs in the light of what has already been established, it is clear that they cannot be regarded as the first stage in the maternal family. Such a view is entirely to mistake the facts. The Nairs are in no respect a people of primitive culture. Through a long period they have most strictly preserved the custom of matriarchal heredity, which has led to an unusual concentration of the family group, and it is probable that here is the best explanation of the conjugal liberty of the Nair girls. However singular their system may appear to us, it is the most logical and complete of any polyandric system. If we compare it with the more usual form of patriarchal polyandry we see at once the influence of maternal descent. Here, the woman makes a free choice of her husbands; in no sense is she their property. It is common for them to work for her, one husband taking on himself to furnish her with clothes, another to give her rice and food, and so on. It is, in fact, the wife who possesses, and it is through her that wealth is transmitted. In fraternal polyandry, on the other hand (as, for instance, it is practised in Thibet and Ceylon), the husbands of a woman are always brothers; she belongs to them, and for her children there is a kind of collective fatherhood. But among the Nairs the man as husband and father cannot be said to exist; he is reduced to the most subordinate rôle of the male — he is simply the progenitor.

I know of no stronger case than this of the degraded position of the father. And what I want to make clear is that in such negation of all father-right rested the inherent weakness in the matriarchal conditions — a weakness which led eventually to the re-establishment of the paternal family. We must be very clear in our minds as to the sharp distinction between the restricted family and the communal clan. The clan as a confederation of members was opposed to the family whose interests were necessarily personal and selfish. Such communism, to some may appear strange at so early a stage of primitive cultures, yet, as I have more than once pointed out, it was a perfectly natural development; it arose through the fierce struggle for existence, forcing the primitive hostile groups to expand and unite with one another for mutual protection. Such conditions of primitive socialism were specially favourable for women. As I have again and again affirmed, the collective motive was more considered by the mothers, and must be sought in the organisation of the maternal clan. But since individual desires can never be wholly subdued, and the male nature is ever directed towards self-assertion, the clan, organised on the rights of the mothers, had always to contend with an opposing force. At one stage the clan was able to absorb the family, but only under exceptional conditions could such a system be maintained. The social organisation of the clan was inevitably broken up as society advanced. With greater security of life the individual interests reasserted their power, and this undermined the dominion of the mother.

To bring these facts home, we must now consider some further examples of mother-right, in order to show how closely these customs are connected with the conditions of the maternal familiar clan.

The Yaos of Africa have what may be regarded as a matriarchal organisation. Kinship is reckoned and property is inherited through the mother. When a man marries, he is expected to live in his wife's village, and his first conjugal duties are to build a house for her, and hoe a garden for her mother. This gives the woman a very important position, and it is she, and not the man, who usually proposes marriage.[107]

In Africa descent through the mother is the rule, though there are exceptions, and these are increasing. The amusing account given by Miss Kingsley[108] of Joseph, a member of the Batu tribe in French Congo, strikingly illustrates the prevalence of the custom. When asked by a French official to furnish his own name and the name of his father, Joseph was wholly nonplussed. "My fader!" he said. "Who my fader?" Then he gave the name of his mother. The case is the same among the negroes. The Fanti of the Gold Coast may be taken as typical. Among them an intensity of affection (accounted for partly by the fact that the mothers have exclusive care of the children) is felt for the mother, while the father is almost disregarded as a parent, notwithstanding the fact that he may be a wealthy and powerful man. The practice of the Wamoimia, where the son of a sister is preferred in legacies, "because a man's own son is only the son of his wife," is typical. The Bush husband does not live with his wife, and often has wives in different places.[109]

In Africa the clan system is firmly established, which explains the prevalence of mother-descent. Women, on the whole, take an important position, and here, as elsewhere, their inheritance of property enables them to maintain their equality with their husbands. Individual possession of wealth is allowed, but a married man usually cannot dispose of any property unless his wife agrees, and she acts as the representative of the children's claims upon the father. The privilege that, according to Laing, the Soulima women have, of leaving their husbands when they please, is also proof of the maternal customs.[110] Moreover, among some tribes, the influence of the mothers as the heads of families extends to the councils of state; it is even said that the chiefs do not decide anything without their consent.[111]

Mother-right is still in force in many parts of India, though owing to the influence of Brahminism on the aboriginal tribes the examples of the maternal family are fewer than might be expected. Among the once powerful Koochs the women own all the property, which is inherited from mother to daughter. The husband lives with his wife and her mother, and, [we are told, is subject to them. These women are most industrious, weaving, spinning, planting and sowing, in a word, doing all the work not above their strength.[112] The Koochs may be compared with the Khasis, already noticed, and these maternal systems among the Indian hill tribes may surely be regarded as showing conditions at one time common. Even tribes who have passed from the clan organisation to the patriarchal family preserve numerous traces of mother-right. Thus, the choice of her lover often remains with the girl;

again, divorce is easy at the wish either of the woman or the man.[113] Such freedom in love is clearly inconsistent with the patriarchal authority of the husband. I must note too the practice, common among many tribes, by which the husband remains in the wife's home for a probationary period, working for her family. This is clearly a step towards purchase marriage, as is proved by the Santals, where this service is claimed when a girl is ugly or deformed and cannot be married otherwise, while other tribes offer their daughters when in want of labourers. This service-marriage must not be confused with the true maternal form, where the bridegroom visits or lives with the wife and any service claimed is a test of his fitness; it shows, however, the power of the woman's kindred still curbing the rights of the husband.[114]

The existence of mother-descent among the peoples of Western Asia has been ascertained with regard to some ancient tribes; but I may pass these over, as they offer no points of special interest. I must, however, refer briefly to the evidence brought forward by the late Prof. Robertson Smith[115] of mother-right in ancient Arabia. We find a decisive example of its favourable influence on the position of women in the custom of *beenah* marriage. Under this maternal form, the wife was not only freed from any subjection involved by the payment of a bride-price in the form of compulsory service or of gifts to her kindred (which always places her more or less under authority), but she was the owner of the tent and the household property, and thus enjoyed the liberty which ownership always entails. This explains how she was able to free herself at pleasure from her husband, who was really nothing but a temporary lover. Ibn Batua, even in the fourteenth century found that the women of Zebid were perfectly ready to marry strangers. The husband might depart when he pleased, but his wife in that case could never be induced to follow him. She bade him a friendly adieu and took upon herself the whole charge of any children of the marriage. The women in Jâhilîya had the right to dismiss their husbands, and the form of dismissal was this: "If they lived in a tent they turned it round, so that if the door faced east it now faced west, and when the man saw this, he knew he was dismissed and did not enter." The tent belonged to the woman: the husband was received there, and at her good pleasure. We find many cases of *beenah* marriage among widely different peoples. Frazer[116] cites an interesting example among the tribes on the north frontier of Abyssinia, partially Semitic peoples, not yet under the influence of Islam, who preserve a maternal marriage closely resembling the *beenah* form, but have as well a purchase marriage, by which a wife is acquired by the payment of a bride-price and becomes the property of her husband.

A very curious form of conjugal contract is recorded among the Hassanyeh Arabs of the White Nile, where the wife passed by contract for a portion of her time only under the authority of her husband. It illustrates in a striking way the conflict in marriage between the old rights of the woman and the rising power of the husband.

> When the parents of the man and the woman meet to settle the price of the woman, the price depends on how many days in the week the marriage tie is to be strictly observed. The woman's mother first of all proposes that, taking everything into consideration, with due regard to the feelings of the family, she could not think of binding her daughter to a due observance of that chastity which matrimony is expected to command for more than two days in the week. After a great deal of apparently angry discussion, and the promise on the part of the relations of the man to pay more, it is arranged that the marriage shall hold good, as is customary among the first families of the tribe, for four days in the week, viz. Monday, Tuesday, Wednesday and Thursday, and in compliance with old established custom, the marriage rites during the three remaining days shall not be insisted on, during which days the bride shall be perfectly free to act as she may think proper, either by adhering to her husband

and home, or by enjoying her freedom and independence from all observance of matrimonial obligations.[117]

A further striking example of mother-right is furnished by the Mariana Islands, where the position of women was distinctly superior.

> Even when the man had contributed an equal share of property on marriage, the wife dictated everything, and the man could undertake nothing without her approval; but if the woman committed an offence, the man was held responsible and suffered the punishment. The women could speak in the assembly; they held property, and if a woman asked anything of a man, he gave it up without a murmur. If a wife was unfaithful, the husband could send her home, keep her property, and kill the adulterer; but if the man was guilty or even suspected of the same offence, the women of the neighbourhood destroyed his house and all his visible property, and the owner was fortunate if he escaped with a whole skin; and if the wife was not pleased with her husband, she withdrew, and a similar attack followed. On this account many men were not married, preferring to live with paid women.[118]

A similar case of the rebellion of men against their position is recorded in Guinea, where religious symbolism was used by the husband as a way of obtaining control and possession of his wife. The maternal system held with respect only to the chief wife.

> It was customary, however, for a man to buy and take to wife a slave, a friendless person with whom he could deal at pleasure, who had no kindred who could interfere with her, and to consecrate her to his Bossum, or god. The Bossum wife, slave as she had been, ranked next to the chief wife, and was exceptionally treated. She alone was very jealously guarded, she alone was sacrificed at her husband's death. She was, in fact, wife in a peculiar sense. And having by consecration been

made of the kindred and worship of her husband her children could be born of his kindred and worship.[119]

It will be readily seen that the special rights held by the husband over these captive-wives would come to be greatly desired. But the capture of women was always difficult, as it frequently led to quarrels and even warfare with the woman's tribe, and for this reason was never widely practised. It would therefore be necessary for another way of escape from the bonds of the maternal marriage to be found. This was done by a system of buying the wife from her clan-kindred, in which case she became the property of her husband.

The change did not, of course, take place at once, and we have many examples of a transition period where the old customs are in conflict with the new. Both forms of marriage, the maternal and the purchase contract, are practised side by side by many peoples. These cases are so instructive that I must add one or two examples to those already noticed. The *ambel-anak* marriage of Sumatra is the maternal form, but there is another marriage known as *djudur*, by which a man buys his wife as his absolute property. There is a complicated system of payments, on which the husband's rights to take the wife to his home depends. If the final sum is paid (but this is not commonly claimed except in the case of a quarrel between the families) the woman becomes to all intents and purposes the slave of the man; but if, on the other hand, as is not at all uncommon, the husband fails or has difficulty in making the main payment, he becomes the debtor of his wife's family, and he is practically the slave, all his labour being due to his wife's family without any reduction in the debt, which must be paid in full, before he regains his liberty.[120] In Ceylon, again, there are two forms of marriage, called *beenah* and *deega*, which cause a marked difference in the position of the wife. A woman married under the *beenah* form lives in the house or immediate neighbourhood of her parents, and if so married she has the right of inheritance along with her brothers; but if married in *deega* she goes to live in her husband's house and village and loses her rights in her own family.[121]

In Africa where the *beenah maternal marriage* is usual, and the husband serves for his wife and lives with her family, it is said that families are usually more or less willing *for value received* to give a woman to a man to take away with him, or to let him have his *beenah* wife to transfer to his own house. Among the Wayao and Mang'anja of the Shirehighlands, south of Lake Nyassa, a man on marrying leaves his own village and goes to live in that of his wife; but, as an alternative, he is allowed to pay a bride-price, in which case he takes his wife away to his home.[122] Again among the Banyai on the Zambesi, if the husband gives nothing the children of the marriage belong to the wife's family, but if he gives so many cattle to his wife's parents the children are his.[123] Similar cases may be found elsewhere. In the Watubela Islands between New Guinea and Celebes a man may either pay for his wife before marriage, or he may, without paying, live as her husband in her parents' house, working for her. In the former case, the children belong to him, in the latter to the mother's family, but he may buy them subsequently at a price.[124] Campbell records of the Limboo tribe (where the bride is usually purchased and lives with the husband), that if poverty compels the bridegroom to serve for his wife, he becomes the slave of her father, "until by his work he has redeemed his bride."[125] An interesting case occurs in some Californian tribes where the husband has to live with the wife and work, until he has paid to her kindred the full price for her and her child. So far has custom advanced in favour of father-right that the children of a wife not paid for are regarded as bastards and held in contempt.[126]

Wherever we find the payment of a bride-price, in whatever form, there is sure indication of the decay of mother-right: woman has become property. Among the Bassa Komo of Nigeria marriage is usually effected by an exchange of sisters or other female relatives. The men may marry as many wives as they have women to give to other men. In this tribe the women look after the children, but the boys, when four years old, go to live and work with the fathers.[127] The husbands of the Bambala tribe (inhabiting the Congo states between the rivers Inzia and Kwilu) have to abstain from visiting their wives for a year after the birth of each child, but they are allowed to return to her on the payment to her father of two goats.[128] Among the Bassanga on the south-west of Lake Moeru the children of the wife belong to the mother's kin, but the children of slaves are the property of the father.

The right of a father to his children was established only by contract. Even where the wife had been given up by her kindred and allowed to live with her husband, we find that the children may be claimed by her family. Thus among the Makolo the price paid on marriage might merely cover the right to have the wife, and in this case the children belonged to the wife's family. It might, however, cover a certain right to the children if that had been contracted for, but never such a right as separated them wholly from the mother's family. To effect this it was necessary that a further price should be paid at the father's death. This sum once paid, her family had "given her up" and her children were entirely severed from them.[129] The legal acknowledgment of fatherhood in all cases had to be paid for.

There are many customs pointing to this new father-force asserting itself, and pushing aside the mother-power. In Africa, among the Bavili the mother has the right to pawn her child, but she must first consult the father, so that he may have a chance of giving her goods to save the pledging.[130] This is very plainly a step towards father-right. There is no distinction between legitimate and illegitimate children. Similar conditions prevail among the Alladians of the Ivory Coast, but here the mother cannot pledge her children without the consent of her brother or other male head of the family. The father has the right to ransom the child.[131] An even stronger example of the property value of children is furnished by the custom found among many tribes, by which the father has to make a present to the wife's family when a child dies: this is called "buying the child."[132] A similar custom prevails among the Maori people of New Zealand; when a child dies, or even meets with an accident, the mother's relations, headed by her brothers, turn out in force against the father. He must defend himself until wounded. Blood once drawn, the combat ceases; but the attacking party plunders his house and appropriates the husband's property, and finally sits down to a feast provided by him.[133]

These cases, with the inferences they suggest, show that the power a husband and father possessed over his wife and her children was gained through purchase. And it is not the fact of the husband's power, however great it might be, that is so important, but the fact that by the change in the form of marriage the wife and her children were cut off from the woman's clan-kindred, whose duty to protect them was now withdrawn. Here, then, was the reason of the change from mother-right to father-right. The monopolist desire of the husband to possess for himself the woman and her children (perhaps the deepest rooted of all the instincts) reasserted itself. But the regaining of this individual possession by man was due, not to male strength, but to purchase. I must insist upon this. As soon as women became sexually marketable their freedom was doomed.

There are many interesting cases of transition in which the children belong sometimes to the mother and sometimes to the father. Again, I can give one or two examples only. In the island of Mangia the parents at the birth of the child arranged between themselves whether it should be dedicated to the father's god or to the mother's. The dedication took place forthwith, and finally determined which parent had the ownership of the child.[134] Among the Haidis, children belong to the clan of the mother, but in exceptional cases when the clan of the father is reduced in numbers, the new-born child may be given to the father's sister to suckle. It is then spoken of as belonging to the paternal aunt and is counted to its father's clan.[135] It is also possible to transfer a child to the father by giving it one of the names common to his clan. There are many curious customs practised by certain tribes, wavering between mother and father descent. In Samoa religion decides the question. At the birth of a child the totem of each parent is prayed to in turn (usually, though not always, starting with that of the father) and whichever totem happens to be invoked at the moment of birth is the child's totem for life and decides whether he or she belongs to the clan of the mother or the father.[136] Equally curious was the custom of the Liburni, where the children were all brought up together until they were five years old. They were then collected and examined in order to trace their likeness to the men and they were assigned to their fathers accordingly. Whoever received a boy from his mother in this way regarded him as his son.[137] Similarly with the Arabs, where one woman was the wife of several men, the custom was either for the woman to decide to which of them the child was to belong, or the child was assigned by an expert to one of the joint husbands to be regarded as his own.[138]

These facts throw a strong light on the bond between the father and the child, which was a legal bond, not dependent, as it is with us, upon blood relationship. Fatherhood really arose out of the ownership of purchase. And for this reason the father's right came to extend to all the children of the wife. It does not appear that the husband makes any distinction between his wife's children, even if they were begotten by other men. Chastity is not regarded as a virtue, and in those cases where unfaithfulness in a wife is punished, it is always because the woman, who has passed from the protection of her kindred, acts without her husband's permission. Interchange of wives is common, while it is one of the duties of hospitality to offer a wife to a stranger guest. Husbands sometimes, indeed, seek other men for their wives, believing they will obtain sons who will excel all others. Thus of the Arabs we are told, there is one form of marriage according to which a man says to his wife, "Send a message to such a one and beg him to have intercourse with you." The husband acts in this way in order that his offspring may be noble.[139] When a Hindu marries, all the children previously born from his wife become his own; in Pakpatan, even when a woman has forsaken her husband for ten years, the children she brings forth are divided between her and her lover.[140] Similarly in Madagascar, when a woman is divorced, any children she afterwards bears belong to her husband.[141] Campbell tells us of children born out of wedlock in the

Limboo tribe that the father may obtain possession of the boys by purchase and by naming them, but the girls belong to the mother.[142]

I am very certain that it was through property considerations and for no moral causes that the stringency of the moral code was tightened for women. It seems to me of very great importance that women should grasp firmly this truth: the virtue of chastity owes its origin to property. Our minds fall so readily under the spell of such ideas as chastity and purity. There is a mass of real superstition on this question — a belief in a kind of magic in chastity. But, indeed, continence had at first no connection with morals. The sense of ownership has been the seed-plot of our moral code. To it we are indebted for the first germs of the sexual inhibitions which, sanctified, by religion and supported by custom, have, under the unreasoned idealism of the common mind, filled life with cruelties and jealous exclusions, with suicides, and murders, and secret shames.[143]

This brings me to summarise the point we have reached. Father-right was dependent on purchase-possession and had nothing to do with actual fatherhood. The payment of a bride-price, the giving of a sister in exchange, as also marriage with a slave, gained for the husband the control over his wife and ownership of the children. I could bring forward much more evidence in proof of this fact that property, and not kinship, was the basis of fatherhood, did the limits of my space allow me to do so; such cases are common in all parts of the world where the transitional stage has been reached. The maternal clan, with its strong social cohesion is then broken up by the growing power of individual interests pushing aside the old customs, and bringing about the restoration of the family. I believe that the causes by which the father gained his position as the dominant partner in marriage must be clear to every one from the examples I have given. Fatherhood established in the first stage of the family on jealous authority, now, after a period of more or less complete obscuration, rises again as the dominant force in marriage. The father has bought back his position as patriarch. On the other hand the mother has lost her freedom that came with the protection of her kindred, under the social organisation of the clan. Looking back through the lengthening record, we find that another step has been taken in the history of the family. This time is it a step forward, or a step backward? This is a question I shall not try to answer, for, indeed, I am not sure.

Yet in case I am mistaken here, let me say at once I am certain that this return to the restricted family was a necessary and inevitable step. The individual forces had to triumph. This may seem a contradiction to all I have just said. What I wish to show is this: one and all the phases in the development of society have been needful and fruitful as successive stages in growth; yet none can continue — none be regarded as the final stage, for each becomes insufficient and narrow from the standpoint of the needs of a later stage. We have reached the third stage — the patriarchal family which still endures. And last and hardest to eradicate is that monopoly of sexual possession, which says: "This woman and her children are mine: I have tabooed her for life." Mankind has still to outlive this brute instinct in its upward way to civilisation.

Women and Primitive Industry

I HAVE REFERRED in an earlier chapter to a letter from Mr H G Wells, sent to me after the publication of my book, *The Truth about Woman*. Now, there is one sentence in this letter that I wish to quote here, because it brings home just what it is my purpose in this chapter to show—that the mother-age was a civilisation owing its institutions, and its early victories over nature, rather to the genius of woman than to that of man. Mr Wells does not, indeed, say this. He rejects the mother-age, and in questioning my acceptance of it as a stage in the past histories of societies, he writes: "The primitive matriarchate never was anything more than mother at the washing-tub and father looking miserable."

It seems to me that here, in his own inimitable way, Mr Wells (though I think quite unconsciously) sums up the past labour-history of woman and man. His statement has very far-reaching considerations. It forces us to accept the active utility of primitive woman in the community — a utility more developed and practical than that of man. This was really the basis of women's position of power. The constructive quality of the female mind, at a time when the male attention and energy were fixed chiefly on the destructive activities of warfare, was liberated for use and invention. Women were the seekers, slowly increasing their efficiency.

Very much the same account of the primitive sexual division in work was given by an Australian Kurnai to Messrs. Fison and Howitt, in a sentence that has been quoted very frequently: "A man hunts, spears fish, fights and sits about, all the rest is woman's work." This may be accepted as a fair statement of how work is divided between the two sexes among primitive peoples. Now, what I wish to make plain is that it was an arrangement in which the advantage was really on the side of the woman rather than on that of the man. I would refer the reader back to what has been said on this subject in Chapter III, where I summed up the conditions acting on the women in the hypothetical first stage of the primordial family. We saw that the males were chiefly concerned with the absorbing duties of sex and fighting rivals, and also hunting for game. The women's interest, on the other hand, was bent on domestic activities — in caring for their children and developing the food supplies immediately around them. From the hearth-home, or shelter, as the start of settled life, and with their intelligence sharpened by the keen chisel of necessity, women carried on their work as the organisers and directors of industrial occupations. Very slowly did they make each far-reaching discovery; seeds cast into the ground sprouted and gave the first start of agriculture. The plant world gave women the best returns for the efforts they made, and they began to store up food. Contrivance followed contrivance, each one making it possible for women to do more. Certain animals, possibly brought back by the hunters from the forests, were kept and tamed. Presently the use of fire was discovered — we know not how — but women became the guardians of this source of life. And now, instead of caves or tree-shelters, there were huts and tents and houses, and of these, too, women were frequently the builders. The home from the first was of greater importance to the women; it was the place where the errant males rejoined their wives and children, and hence the women became the owners of the homes and the heads of households. For as yet the men were occupied in fighting. The clumsy and the stupid among them were killed soonest; the fine hand, the quick eye — these prevailed age by age. Tools and weapons were doubtless fashioned by these fighters, but for destruction; the male's attention was directed mainly by his own desires. And may we not accept that among the most pressing activities of women was the need to tame man and make him social, so that he could endure the rights of others than himself?

So through the long generations the life of human societies continued. Those activities, due to female influence, developing and opening up new ways in all directions, until we have that early civilisation, which I have called the mother-age.

All the world over, even to this day, this separation in the labour activities of the two sexes can be traced. Destructive work, demanding a special development of strength, with corresponding periods of rest, falls to men; and contrasted with this violent and intermittent male force we find, with the same uniformity, that the work of women is domestic and constructive, being connected with the care of children and all the various industries which radiate from the home — work demanding a different kind of strength, more enduring, more continuous, but at a lower tension.

Bonwick's account of the work of Tasmanian women may be taken as typical:

> In addition to the necessary duty of looking after the children, the women had to provide all the food for the household excepting that derived from the chase of the kangaroo. They climbed up hills for the opossum" (a very difficult task, requiring great strength and also skill), "delved in the ground for yams, native bread, and nutritious roots, groped about the rocks for shellfish, dived beneath the sea for oysters, and fished for the finny tribe. In addition to this, they carried, on their frequent tramps, the household stuffs in native baskets of their own manufacture.[144]

Among the Indians of Guiana the men's work is to hunt, and to cut down the trees when the cassava is to be planted. When the men have felled the trees and cleaned the ground, the women plant the cassava and undertake all the subsequent operations; agriculture is entirely in their hands. They are little, if at all, weaker than the men, and they work all day while the men are often in their hammocks smoking; but there is no cruelty or oppression exercised by the men towards the women.[145]

In Africa we meet with much the same conditions of labour. "The work is done chiefly by the women, this is universal; they hoe the fields, sow the seed, and reap the harvest. To them, too, falls all the labour of house-building, grinding corn, brewing beer, cooking, washing, and caring for almost all the material interests of the community. The men tend the cattle, hunt, go to war; they also spend much time sitting in council over the conduct of affairs."[146]

I may note the interesting account of Prof Haddon[147] of the work of the Western Tribes of the Torres Straits:

> The men fished, fought, built houses, did a little gardening, made fish-lines, fish-hooks, spears, and other implements, constructed dance-masks and head-dresses, and all the paraphernalia for the various ceremonies and dances. They performed all the rites and dances, and in addition did a good deal of strutting up and down, loafing and 'yarning.' The women cooked and prepared the food, did most of the gardening, collected shellfish, and speared fish on the reefs, made petticoats, baskets and mats.

Similar examples might be almost indefinitely multiplied. Among the Andamanese, while the men go into the jungle to hunt pigs, the women fetch drinking water and firewood, catch shell-fish, make fishing nets and baskets, spin thread, and cook the food ready for the return of the men.[148] The Moki women of America have fifty ways of preparing corn for food. They make all the preparations necessary for these varied dishes, involving the arts of the stonecutter, the carrier, the mason, the miller and the cook.[149] In New Caledonia "girls work in the plantations, boys learn to fight."[150]

We should, however, fall into a popular error concerning the division of labour in savagery, if we consider that all women's work is regarded as degrading to men and all men's work is tabooed to women. The duties of war and the chase are the chief occupation of men, yet in all parts of the world women have fought at need, and sometimes habitually, both to assist their men and also against them. Thus Buckley, who lived for many years among the Australian tribes, relates that when the tribe he lived with was attacked by a hostile party, the men "raised a war-cry; on hearing this the women threw off their rugs and, each armed with a short club, flew to the assistance of their husbands and brothers."[151] In Central Australia the men occasionally beat the women through jealousy, but on such occasions it is by no means rare for the women, single handed, to beat the men severely.[152] Again, men carry on, as a rule, the negotiations on tribal concerns, but in such matters exceptions are very numerous. Among the Australian Dieyerie, Curr states that the women act as ambassadors to arrange treaties, and invariably succeed in their mission.[153] The same conditions are found among the American Indians. Men are the hunters and fishers, but women also hunt and fish. Among the Yahgan of Tierra del Fuego fishing is left entirely to the women,[154] and this is not at all unusual. Mrs Allison states of the Similkameen Indians of British Columbia that formerly "the women were nearly as good hunters as the men," but being sensitive to the ridicule of the white settlers, they have given up hunting.[155] In hunting trips, the help of women is often not to be despised. Warburton Pike writes thus: "I saw what an advantage it is to take women on a hunting trip. If we killed anything, we had only to cut up and *cache* the meat, and the women would carry it. On returning to camp we could throw ourselves down on a pile of caribou skins and smoke our pipes in comfort, but the women's work was never finished."[156] This account is very suggestive. The man undergoes the fatigue of hunting, and when he has thrown the game at the woman's feet his part is done; it is her duty to carry it and to cook it, as well as to make the vessels in which the food is placed. The skins and the refuse are hers to utilise, and all the industries connected with clothing are chiefly in her hands.[157] Hearne, in his delightful old narrative, speaks of the assistance of women on hunting expeditions:

> For when all the men are heavy laden they can neither hunt nor travel to any considerable distance; and in case they meet with any success in hunting, who is to carry the produce of their labour?

He adds with a charming frankness:

> Women were made for labour; one of them can carry or haul as much as two men can do. They also pitch our tents, make and mend our clothing, keep us warm at night, and, in fact, there is no such thing as travelling any considerable distance, or any length of time, in this country without their assistance.[158]

Numerous other examples might be added which illustrate how women take part in the destructive work of men; conversely we find not a few cases of the cooperation of men in the women's activities. The world over, women are usually the weavers and spinners; but with the Navajo and in some of the Pueblos the men are among the best weavers.[159] Among the Indians of Guiana the men are specially skilful in basket-weaving, and here also they as well as the women spin and weave.[160] More curious is the custom in East Africa where all the sewing for their own and the women's garments is done by the men, and very well done. Sewing is here so entirely recognised as men's work that a wife may obtain a divorce if she "can show a neglected rend in her petticoat."[161]

It is a common mistake, arising from insufficient knowledge, to suppose that savage women are specially subject to oppression. Their life is hard as we look at it, but not as they look at it. We have still much to learn on these matters. An even greater error is the view that these women are a source of weakness to the male members of their families. The very reverse is the truth. Primitive women are strong in body and capable in work. Fison and Howitt, in discussing this question, state of the Australian women, "In times of peace, they are the hardest workers and the most useful members of the community." And in times of war, "they are perfectly capable of taking care of themselves at all times, and so far from being an encumbrance on the warriors, they will fight, if need be, as bravely as the men, and with even greater ferocity."[162] This is no exceptional case. The strength of savage women is proved by reports from widely different races, of which all testify to their physical capability and aptness for labour. Schellong,[163] who has carefully studied the Papuans of the German protectorate of New Guinea, from the anthropological point of view, "considers that the women are more strongly built than the men." Nor does heavy work appear to damage the health or beauty of the women, but the contrary. Thus among the Andombies on the Congo, to give one instance, the women, though working very hard as carriers, and as labourers in general, lead an entirely happy existence; they are often stronger than the men and more finely developed: some of them, we are told, have really splendid figures. And Parke, speaking of the Manyuema of the Arruwimi in the same region, says that "they are fine animals, and the women very handsome; they carry loads as heavy as those of the men and do it quite as well."[164] Again, McGee[165] comments on the extraordinary capacity of quite aged women for heavy labour. He tells of "a withered crone, weighing apparently not more than 80 to 90 lb who carried a *kilio* containing a stone mortar 196 lb in weight for more than half a mile on a sandy road without any perceptible exhaustion. The proportion of the active aged is much larger than among civilised people."

I may pause to note some of the numerous industries of which women were the originators. First of all, woman is the food-giver; all the labours relating to the preparation of food, and to the utilisation of the side products of foodstuffs are usually found in the hands of women. Women are everywhere the primitive agriculturists. They beat out the seeds from plants; dig for roots and tubers, strain the poisonous juices from the cassava and make bread from the residue; and it was under their attention that a southern grass was first developed into what we know as Indian corn.[166] The removal of poisonous matter from tapioca by means of hot water is also the discovery of savage women.[167] All the evolution of primitive agriculture may be traced to women's industry. Power tells of the Yokia women in Central California who employ neither plough nor hoe, but cultivate the ground by digging the earth deep and rubbing it fine with their hands, and by this means they get an excellent yield.[168] Women have everywhere been the first potters; vessels were needed for use in cooking, to carry and to hold water, and to store the supplies of food. For the same reason baskets were woven. Women invented and exercised in common multifarious household occupations and industries. Curing food, tanning the hides of animals, spinning, weaving, dyeing — all are carried on by women. The domestication of animals is usually in women's hands. They are also the primitive architects; the hut, in widely different parts of the world — among Kaffirs, Fuegians, Polynesians, Kamtschatdals — is built by women. We have seen that the communal houses of the American Indians are mainly erected by the women. Women were frequently, though not always, the primitive doctors. Among the Kurds, for instance, all the medical knowledge is in the hands of the women, who are the hereditary *hakims*.[169] Women seem to have prepared the first intoxicating liquors. The Quissama women in Angola climb the gigantic palm trees to obtain palm-beer.[170] In the ancient legends of the North, women are clearly represented as the discoverers of ale.[171]

It would be easy to go on almost indefinitely multiplying examples of the industries of primitive women. There can be no doubt at all that their work is exacting and incessant; it is also inventive in its variety and its ready application to the practical needs of life. If a catalogue of the primitive forms of labour were made, each woman would be found doing at least half-a-dozen things while a man did one. We may accept the statement of Prof Mason that in the early history of mankind "women were the industrial, elaborative, conservative half of society. All the peaceful arts of today were once women's peculiar province. Along the lines of industrialism she was pioneer, inventor, author, originator."[172]

There is another matter that must be noted. The primitive division of labour between the sexes was not in any sense an arrangement dictated by men, nor did they impose the women's tasks upon them. The view that the women are forced to work by the laziness of the men, and that their heavy and incessant labour is a proof of their degraded position is entirely out of focus. Quite the reverse is the truth. Evidence is not wanting of the great advantage arising to women from their close connection with labour. It was largely their control over the food supply and their position as actual producers which gave them so much influence, and even authority in the mother-age. In this connection I may quote the statement of Miss Werner about the African women as representing the true conditions:

> I cannot say that, so far as my own observations went, the women's lot seemed to be a specially hard one. In fact, they are too important an element in the community not to be treated with consideration. The fact that they do most of the heavy field-work does not imply that they are a down-trodden sex. On the contrary, it gives them a considerable pull, as a man will think twice before endangering his food supply."[173]

Mr Horatio Hale, a well-known American anthropologist likewise observes:

> The common opinion that women among savage tribes in general are treated with harshness, and regarded as slaves, or at least as inferiors, is, like many common opinions, based on error, originating in too large and indiscriminate deduction from narrow premises.... The wife of a Samoan landowner or Navajo shepherd has no occasion, so far as her position in her family or among her people, to envy the wife of a German peasant.[174]

Certainly savage women do not count their work as any

degradation. There is really an equal division of labour between the sexes, though the work of the men is accomplished more fitfully than that of the women. The militant activities of fighting and hunting are essential in primitive life. The women know this, and they do their share — the industrial share, willingly, without question, and without compulsion. It is entirely absurd in this work-connection to regard men as the oppressors of women. Rather the advantage is on the women's side. For one thing, just because they are accustomed to hard labour all their lives, they are little, if any, weaker than men. Primitive women are strong in body, and capable in work. The powers they enjoy as well as their manifold activities are the result of their position as mothers, this function being to them a source of strength and not a plea of weakness.

"They who are accustomed to the ways of civilised women only," remarks Mr Fison, "can hardly believe what savage women are capable of, even when they may well be supposed to be at their weakest. For instance, an Australian tribe on the march scarcely take the trouble to halt for so slight a performance as childbirth. The newly born infant is wrapped in skins, the march is resumed, and the mother trudges on with the rest. Moreover, as is well known, among many tribes elsewhere it is the father who is put to bed, while the mother goes about her work as if nothing had happened."[175]

Another important advantage arising to women, through their identification with the early industrial process, was their position as the first property owners. They were almost the sole creators of ownership in land, and held in this respect a position of great power. This explains the fact that in the transactions of the North American tribes with the Colonial Government many deeds of assignment bear female signatures.[176] A form of divorce used by a husband in ancient Arabia was: "Begone, for I will no longer drive thy flocks to pasture."[177] In almost all cases the household goods belonged to the woman. The stores of roots and berries laid up for a time of scarcity were the property of the wife, and the husband would not touch them without her permission. In many cases such property was very extensive. Among the Menomini Indians, for instance, a woman of good circumstances would own as many as 1200 to 1500 birch-bark vessels.[178] In the New Mexico Pueblos what comes from the outside of the house as soon as it is inside is put under the immediate control of the women. Bandelier, in his report of his tour in Mexico, tells us that "his host at Cochiti, New Mexico, could not sell an ear of corn or a string of chili without the consent of his fourteen-year-old daughter, Ignacia, who kept house for her widowed father."[179]

I must now bring this brief chapter to a close. But first I would give one further example. It is an account of the Pelew matrons' work in the taro fields. Here the richest and most influential women count it their privilege to labour, and it will be remembered that these women are called "mothers of the land." They are politically and socially superior to the men; and their position is dependent largely on their close connection with the staple industry of the island.

> The richest woman in the village looks with pride on her taro patch, and although she has female followers enough to allow her merely to superintend the work without taking part in it, she nevertheless prefers to lay aside her fine apron, and to betake herself to the field, merely clad in a small apron that barely hides her nakedness, with a little mat on her back to protect her from the burning heat of the sun, and with a shade of banana leaves for her eyes. There, dripping with sweat in the burning sun, and coated with mud to the hips and over the elbows, she toils to set the younger women a good example. Moreover, as in every other occupation, the *Kalitho,* the gods must be invoked, and who could be better fitted for the discharge of so important a duty than 'the Mother of the House.'

Here is a picture of labour that may well make women pause to think.

Traces of Mother-Right Customs in Ancient and Modern Civilisations

I PROPOSE IN this chapter to examine, as fully as I can, the traces that mother-right customs have left among some of the great races of antiquity, as also in the early records of western civilisations. It is the more necessary to do this because there is so marked a tendency to minimise the importance of the mother-age, and to regard the patriarchal family as primeval and universal. So much interesting material is available, and so wide a field of inquiry must be covered, that I shall be able to give a mere outline sketch, for the purpose of suggesting, rather than proving, the widespread prevalence of the communal clan and the maternal family.

As to whether this maternal-stage, with kinship and inheritance passing through the mother, has everywhere preceded the second patriarchal period, it is difficult to be at all certain. Dr Westermarck, Mr Crawley and others have argued against this view. But (as I have before had occasion to point out) their chief motive has been to discredit the theory of promiscuity, with which mother-descent has been so commonly, and so mistakenly, connected. It does not seem to have been held as possible that the mother-age was a much later development, whose social customs were made for the regulation of the family relationships. A number of very primitive races exhibit no traces, that have yet been discovered, of such a system, and have descent in the male line. This has been thought to be a further proof against a maternal stage. But here again is an error; we are not entitled to regard mother-descent as necessarily the primitive custom. I believe and have tried to show, from the examples of the Australian tribes and elsewhere, that in many cases the stage of the maternal clan has not been reached. If I am right here, we have the way cleared from much confusion. I would suggest, as also possible, that there may among some people, have been retrogressions, customs and habits found out as beneficial, and perhaps for long practised, have by some tribes been forgotten. There can be no hard and fast rule of progress for any race. The whole subject is thorny and obscure, and the evidence on the question is often contradictory. Still I hold the claim I make is not without foundation. I have tried to show how the causes which led to the maternal system were perfectly simple and natural causes, arising out of needs that must have operated universally in the past history of mankind. And this indicates a maternal stage at some period for all branches of the human family. Again the widespread prevalence of mother-right survivals among races where the patriarchal system has been for long firmly established lends support to such a view, which will be strengthened by the evidence now to be brought forward. It will be necessary to go step by step, from one race to another, and to many different countries, and I would ask my readers not to shrink from the trouble of following me.

Let us turn first to ancient Egypt, where women held a position more free and more honourable than they have in any country today.

Herodotus, who was a keen observer, records his astonishment at this freedom, and writes —

> They have established laws and customs opposite for the most part to those of the rest of mankind.... With them women go to market and traffic; men stay at home and weave.... The men carry burdens on their heads; the women on their shoulders.... The boys are never forced to maintain their parents unless they wish to do so; the girls are obliged to, even if they do not wish it.[180]

From this last rule it is logical to infer that women inherited property, as is today the case among the Beni-Amer of Africa, where daughters have to provide for their parents.[181]

Diodorus goes further than Herodotus: he affirms that in the Egyptian family it is the man who is subjected to the woman.

> All this explains why the queen receives more power and respect than the king, and why, among private individuals, the woman rules over the man, and that it is stipulated between married couples, by the terms of the dowry-contract, that the man shall obey the woman.[182]

There is probably some exaggeration in this account, nevertheless, the demotic deeds, in a measure, confirm it. By the law of maternal inheritance, an Egyptian wife was often richer than her husband, and enjoyed the dignity and freedom always involved by the possession of property. More than three thousand three hundred years ago men and women were recognised as equal in this land.

Under such privileges the wife was entirely preserved from any subjection; she was able to dictate the terms of the marriage. She held the right of making contracts without authorisation; she remained absolute mistress of her dowry. The marriage-contract also specified the sums that the husband was to pay to his wife, either as a nuptial gift or annual pension, or as compensation in case of divorce. In some cases the whole property of the husband was made over to the wife, and when this was done, it was stipulated that she should provide for him during his life, and discharge the expenses of his burial and tomb.

These unusual proprietary rights of the Egyptian wife can be explained only as being traceable to an early period of mother-right. Without proof of any absolutely precise text, we have an accumulation of facts that render it probable that, at one time, descent was traced through the mother. It is significant that the word *husband* never occurs in the marriage deeds before the reign of Philometor. This ruler (it would appear in order to establish the position of the father in the family) decreed that all transfers of property made by the wife should henceforth be authorised by the husband. Up to this time public deeds often mention only the mother, but King Philometor ordered the names of contractors to be registered according to the paternal line. Besides this, the hieroglyphic funeral inscriptions frequently bear the name of the mother, without indicating that of the father.[183]

All these facts attest that women in Egypt enjoyed an exceptionally favourable position. We may compare this position with that held by the Touareg women of the Sahara, who, through the custom of maternal inheritance, for long continued, have in their hands the strong power of wealth, and thus exercise extraordinary authority, giving rise to what I have called "a pecuniary matriarchy."

It is probable that in Egypt property was originally entirely in the hands of women, as is usual under the matriarchal system. Later, a tradition in favour of the old privileges would seem to have persisted after descent was changed from the maternal to the paternal line. The marriage-contracts may thus be regarded as enforcing by agreement what would occur naturally under the maternal customs. The husband's property was made over by deed to the wife (at first entirely, and afterwards in part) to secure its inheritance by the children of the marriage. It was in such wise way the Egyptians arranged the difficult problem of the fusing of mother-right with father-right.

In the very ancient civilisation of Babylon we find women in a position of honour, with privileges similar in many ways to those they enjoyed in Egypt. There are even indications that the earliest customs may have gone beyond those of the Egyptians in exalting women. All the available evidence points to the conclusion that at the opening of Babylonian history women had complete independence and equal rights with their husbands and brothers. It is significant that the most archaic texts in the primitive language are remarkable for the precedence given to the female sex in all formulas of address: "Goddesses and gods;" "Women and men," are mentioned always in that order; this is in itself a decisive indication of the high status of women in this early period. And there are other traces all pointing to the conclusion that in the civilisation of primitive Babylon mother-right was still in active force. Later (as is shown by the Code of Hammurabi) a woman's rights, though not her duties, were more circumscribed; in the still later Neo-Babylonian periods, she again acquired, through the favourable conditions with regard to property, full liberty of action and equal rights with her husband.[184]

Let us now turn our attention to the Greco-Roman civilisation. It is convenient to take first a brief glance at Rome. I may note that the family here would certainly appear to have developed from the primitive clan, or *gens*. At the dawn of history the patriarchal system was already firmly established, with individual property, and an unusually strong subjection of woman to her father first and afterwards to her husband. There are, however, numerous indications of a prehistoric phase of communism. I can mention only the right of the *gens* to the heritage, and in certain cases the possession of an *ager publicus*, which certainly bears witness in favour of an antique community of property.[185] Can we, then, accept that there was once a period of the maternal family, when descent and inheritance were traced through the mother? Frazer[186] has brought forward facts which point to the view that the Roman kingship was transmitted in the female line; and, if this can be accepted, we may fairly conclude that at one time the maternal customs were in force. The plebeian marriage ceremonies of Rome should be noted. The funeral inscriptions in Etruria in the Latin language make much greater insistence on the maternal than the paternal descent; giving usually the name of the mother alone, or indicating the father's name by a simple initial, whilst that of the mother is written in full.[187] This is very significant. Very little trustworthy evidence, however, is forthcoming, and of the position of women in Rome in the earliest periods we know little or nothing. And for this reason I shall refer my readers to what I have written elsewhere[188] on this matter; merely saying that there are indications and traditions pointing to the view that here, as in so many great civilisations, women's actions were once unfettered, and this, as I believe, can be explained only on the hypothesis of the existence of a maternal stage, before the establishment of the individual male authority under the patriarchal system.

The evidence with regard to prehistoric Greece is much more complete. The Greek ã?îiò resembled the Roman *gens.* Its members had a common sepulture, common property, the mutual obligation of the *vendetta* and archon.[189] In the prehistoric clans maternal descent would seem to have been established. Plutarch relates that the Cretans spoke of Crete as their motherland, and not fatherland. In primitive Athens, the women had the right of voting, and their children bore their name — privileges that were taken from them, says the legend, to appease the wrath of Poseidon, after his inundation of the city, owing to the quarrel with Athene. Tradition also relates that at Athens, until the time of Cecrops, children bore the name of their mother.[190] Among the Lycians, whose affinity to the Greeks was so pronounced, a matriarchate prevailed down to the time of Herodotus. Not the name only, but the inheritance and status of the children depended on the mother. The Lycians "honoured women rather than men;" they are represented "as being accustomed from of old to be ruled by their women."[191]

One of the most remarkable instances of a gynaecocratic people has only now been fully discovered as having existed in ancient Crete. It seems probable that women enjoyed greater powers than they had even in Egypt. The new evidence that has come to light is certainly most interesting; the facts are recorded by Mr J R Hall in a recent book, *Ancient History in the Far East,* and I am specially glad to bring them forward. He affirms: "It may eventually appear that in religious matters, perhaps even the government of the State itself as well, were largely controlled by the women." From the seals we gather a universal worship of a supreme female goddess, the Rhea of later religions, who is accompanied sometimes by a youthful male deity. Wherever we find this preponderating feminine principle in worship we shall find also a corresponding feminine influence in the customs of the people. We have seen this, for instance, among the Khasis, where also goddesses are placed before gods. Mr Hall further states: "It is certain that they [the women in Crete] must have lived on a footing of greater equality with men than in any other ancient civilisation." And again: "We see in the frescoes of Knossos conclusive indications of an open and free association of men and women, corresponding to our idea of 'Society,' at the Minoan court, unparalleled till our own day." The women are unveiled, and the costumes and setting are extraordinarily modern. Mr Hall draws attention to the curious fact that in appearance the women are very similar to the men, so that often the sexes can be distinguished only by the conventions of the artists, representing the women in white, and the men in red outline; the same convention that was used in Egypt. I may recall to the reader the likeness of the men to the women among the North American Indians, and the same similarity between the sexes occurs among the ancient Egyptians.[192] It is perhaps impossible to search for an explanation. I would, however, point out that in all these cases, where the sexes appear to be more alike than is common, we find women in a position of equality with men. This is really very remarkable; I think it is a fact that demands more attention than as yet it has received.

At one time there would seem to have been in prehistoric Greece a period of fully established mother-right. Ancient Attic traditions are filled with recollections of female supremacy. Women in the Homeric legends hold a position and enjoy a freedom wholly at variance with a patriarchal subjection. Not infrequently the husband owes to his wife his rank and his wealth; always the wife possesses a dignified place and much influence. Even the formal elevation of women to positions of authority is not uncommon. "There is nothing," says Homer, "better and nobler than when husband and wife, being of one mind, rule a household. Penelope and Clytemnestra were left in charge of the realms of their husbands during their absence in Troy; the beautiful Chloris ruled as queen in Pylos. Arete, the beloved wife of Alcinous played an important part as peacemaker in the kingdom of her husband."[193]

If we turn to the evidence of the ancient mythology and art, it is also clear that the number of female deities must be connected with the early predominance of women in Greece. We have to remember that "the gods" are shaped by human beings in their own image, and the status of women on earth is reflected in the status of a goddess. Five out of the eight divinities of immemorial Greek worship were female, Hera, Demeter, Persephone, Athene and Aphrodite. In addition there were numerous lesser goddesses. One must consider also that it was not uncommon for cities to be named after women; and the Greek stories seem to point to tribes with totem names. How can these things be explained, unless we accept a maternal stage? There are numerous other facts all indicating this same conclusion. We find relationships on the mother's side regarded as much more close than those on the father's side. In Athens and Sparta a man might marry his father's sister, but not his mother's sister. Lycaon, in pleading with Achilles, says in order to appease him, that he is not the uterine brother of Hector. It is also noteworthy to find that the Thebans, when pressed in war, seek assistance from the Aeginetans as their nearest kin, *recollecting that Thebe and Aeginia had been sisters.* A similar case is that of the Lycaones in Crete, who claimed affinity with Athens and with Sparta, which affinity was traced through the mother.[194]

There is much evidence I am compelled to pass over. It must, however, be noted that there seems clear proof of the maternal form of marriage having at one time been practised. Plutarch mentions that the relations between husband and wife in Sparta were at first secret.[195] The story told by Pausanias about Ulysses' marriage certainly points to the custom of the bridegroom going to live with the wife's family.[196] In this connection the action of Intaphernes is significant, who, when granted by Darius permission to claim the life of a single man, chose her brother, saying that both husband and children could be replaced.[197] Similarly the declaration of Antigone that neither for husband nor children would she have performed the toil she undertook for Polynices[198] clearly shows that the tie of the common womb was held as closer than the tie of marriage; and this points to the conditions of the communal clan.

Andromache, when she relates to Hector how her father's house has been destroyed, with all who are in it, turns to him and says: "But now, Hector, thou art my father and gracious mother, thou art my brother, nay, thou art my valiant husband."[199] It is easy, I think, to see in this speech how the early idea of the relationships under mother-right had been transferred to the husband, as the protector of the woman conditioned by father-right. As in so many countries, the patriarchal authority of the husband does not seem to have existed in Greece at this early stage of development. It may, however, be said that all this, though proving the high status of women in the prehistoric period, does not establish the existence of the maternal family. I would ask: how, then, are these mother-right customs to be explained? In the later history of Greece, with the family based on patriarchal authority, all this was changed. We find women occupying a much less favourable position, their rights and freedom more and more restricted. In Sparta alone, where the old customs for long were preserved, did the women retain anything of their old dignity and influence. The Athenian wives, under the authority of their husbands, sank almost to the level of slaves.[200]

The patriarchal system is connected closely in our thought with the Hebrew family, where the father, who is chief, holds grouped under his despotic sway his wives, their children, and slaves. Yet this Semitic patriarch has not existed from the beginning; numerous survivals of mother-right customs afford proof that the Hebrew race must have passed through a maternal stage. These survivals have a special interest, as we are all familiar with them in Bible history, but we have not understood their significance. It is possible to give a few illustrations only. In the history of Jacob's service for his wives, we have clear proof of the maternal custom of *beenahh* marriage. As a suitor Jacob had to buy his position as husband and to serve Laban for seven years before he was permitted to marry Leah, and seven years for Rachel, while six further years of service were claimed before he was allowed the possession of his cattle.[201] Afterwards, when he wished to depart with his wives and his children, Laban made the objection, "these daughters are my daughters, and these children are my children."[202] Now, according to the patriarchal custom, Laban's daughters should have been cut off from their father by marriage, and become of the kindred of their husbands. Such a claim on the part of the father proves the subordinate position held by the husband in the wife's family, who retained control over her and the children of the marriage, and even over the personal property of the man, as was usual under the later matriarchal custom. Even when the marriage is not in the maternal form, and the wife goes to the husband's home, we find compensation has to be paid to her kindred. Thus when Abraham sought a wife for Isaac, presents were taken by the messenger to induce the bride to leave her home; and these presents were given not to the father of the bride, but to her mother and brother.[203] This is the early form of purchase marriage, such bridal-gifts being the forerunners of the payment of a fixed bride-price. We still find purchase marriage practised side by side with *beenah* marriage in the countries where the transitional stage has been reached and mother-right contends with father-right. But there is stronger evidence even than these two cases. The injunction in Gen. ii, 24: "Therefore shall a man leave his father and his mother, and shall cleave unto his wife," refers without any doubt to the early form of marriage under mother-right, when the husband left his own kindred and went to live with his wife and among her people. We find Samson visiting his Philistine wife who remained with her own people.[204] Even the obligation to blood vengeance rested apparently on the maternal kinsmen (Judges viii, 19). The Hebrew father did not inherit from the son, nor the grandfather from the grandson, which points back to a time when the children did not belong to the clan of the father.[205] Among the Hebrews individual property was instituted at a very early period,[206] but various customs show clearly the early existence of communal clans. Thus the inheritance, especially the paternal inheritance, must remain in the clan "then shall their inheritance be added unto the inheritance of the tribe." Marriage in the tribe is obligatory for daughters. "Let them marry to whom they think best; only to the family of the tribe of their father shall they marry. So shall no inheritance of the children of Israel remove from tribe to tribe."[207] We have here an indication of the close relation between father-right and property.

Under mother-right there is naturally no prohibition against marriage with a half-sister upon the father's side. This explains the marriage of Abraham with Sarah, his half-sister by the same father. When reproached for having passed his wife off as his sister to the King of Egypt, the patriarch replies: "For indeed she is my sister; she is the daughter of my father, but not the daughter of my mother, and she became my wife."[208] In the same way Tamar could have married her half-brother Amnon, though they were both the children of David: "Speak to the King, for he will not withhold me from thee." And it was her uterine brother, Absalom, who revenged the rape of Tamar by slaying; afterwards he fled to the kindred of his mother.[209] Again, the father of Moses and Aaron married his father's sister, who legally was not considered to be related to him.[210] Nabor, the brother of Abraham, took to wife his fraternal niece, the daughter of his brother.[211] It was only later that paternal kinship became legally recognised among the Hebrews by the same titles as the natural kinship through the mother.

It is by considering these survivals of mother-right in connection with similar customs to be found among existing maternal peoples that we see their true significance. They warrant us in believing that the patriarchal family, as we know it among the Hebrews and elsewhere, was a later stage of an evolution, which had for its starting-point the communal clan, and that these races have passed through the maternal phase. We come to understand the change in the privileged position of women. As the husband and father continued to gain in power, with the reassertion of individual interests, it was inevitable that the mother should lose the authority she had held, under the free social organisation of the undivided clan.

Traces of a similar evolution of the family may, I am convinced, be found by all who will undertake an inquiry for themselves. The subject is one of great interest. So far as my own study goes, I believe that these survivals of the maternal-group customs may be discovered in the early history of every people, where the necessary material for such knowledge is available. I wish it were possible for me even to summarise all the evidence, direct and inferential, that I have collected for my own satisfaction. I must reluctantly pass over many countries I would like to include; some of these — China, Japan, Burma and Madagascar — have been noticed briefly in *The Truth about Woman*.[212] There is surprising similarity between the facts; and, the more of such survivals that can be found, the more the evidence seems to grow in favour of the acceptance of a universal maternal stage in the evolution of society.

I must now, before closing this chapter (whose accumulation of facts may, I fear, have wearied my readers), refer briefly to the races of barbarous Europe. The point of interest is, of course — how far mother-right may be accepted, as at one period, having existed. The earliest direct evidence is the account given by Strabo of the Iberians of ancient Spain. And first it is important to note that the Iberians belonged to the Berber race, now widely regarded as the parent of the chief and largest element in the population of Europe. There is another fact that must be noted. The general characteristic of the Berber family seems to have been the privileged position they accorded to their women, privileges so great that we meet with strong tendencies towards the matriarchate. This last is still in force among the Touaregs of the Sahara; and there are as well numerous traces of its former existence among the neighbouring Kabyles, though there the most rigorous patriarchate has replaced the maternal family.[213] We have seen, too, that in ancient Egypt, where the Berbers were largely represented, women enjoyed a position of extraordinary freedom and authority.

Bearing this in mind, we may accept the statement of Strabo: "Among the Cantabrians usage requires that the husband shall bring a dower to his wife, and the daughters inherit, being charged with the marriage of their brothers, which constitutes a kind of gynaecocracy." There is possibly some exaggeration in the term gynaecocracy; yet if there is no proof of "rule by women," there can be no doubt that, through the system of female inheritance, property was held by them, and this must certainly have given them the power always involved by the possession of wealth.

The freedom of the women of ancient Spain is sufficiently indicated by the fact that they took part in the activities usually considered as belonging to men. It was these women who played their part in driving back the Roman legions from the mountainous districts of northern Spain; we read of them fighting side by side with men, where they used their weapons with courage and determination. They received their wounds with silent fortitude, and no cry of pain ever escaped their lips, even when the wounds which laid them low were mortal. To women as well as men liberty was a possession more valued than life, and, when taken prisoners, they fell upon their own swords, and dashed their little ones to death rather than suffer them to live to be slaves. Nor were the activities of women confined to warfare. Justin speaks of women as not only having the care of all domestic matters, but also cultivating the fields. And Strabo, writing of these Amazons, tells us that they would often step aside out of the furrows "to be brought to bed," and then, having borne a child, would return to their work "just as if they had only laid an egg." He notes, too, as being practised among them the *couvade*, whereby the husband, in assertion of his legal fatherhood, retired to bed when a child was born.[214]

Spain is a land that I know well, and for this reason I have chosen to write of it in fuller detail. Persistent relics of the early maternal period even yet may be traced in the customs of this strongly conservative people. Women are held in honour. There is a proverb common all over Spain to the effect that "he who is unfortunate and needs assistance should seek his mother." Many primitive customs survive, and one of the most interesting is that by which the eldest daughter in some cases takes precedence over the sons in inheritance. Among the Basques, until quite recently, the administration of the family property passed to the eldest child, whether a boy or a girl; and in the case of a daughter, her husband was obliged to take the name of the family and to live in the wife's home. Spanish women always retain their own names after marriage, and as far back as the fourth century we find them at the Synod of Elvira resisting an attempt to limit this freedom. The practice is still common for children to use the name of the mother coupled with that of the father, and even, in some cases, alone, showing a quite unusual absence of preference for paternal descent. This is very significant. It explains the recognition given in old Spain to the unmarried mother; even today in no country, that I know, does less social stigma fall on a child born out of wedlock. The profound Spanish veneration of the Virgin Mary, as well as the number of female saints, is another indication of the honour paid to women, which must, I am certain, be connected with a far back time when goddesses were worshipped. I would note, too, the fine Spanish understanding of hospitality. This belongs to the ideals of communal life. I know nothing to equal it in the common habits of other European countries. It may be compared with the conditions in the joint-family communities of the American Indians.[215]

Much more might be said on the position of the Spanish women. I have, however, written elsewhere of these women,[216] of their intelligence, and strength, and beauty, and of the active part they take still in the industrial life of the country. There can be no question that some features of the maternal customs have left their imprint on the domestic life of Spain, and this, as I believe, explains how women here have in certain directions, preserved a freedom of action and privileges, which even in England have never been established, and only of late claimed.

As we may expect, there is less direct evidence of mother-right in the other European countries than is the case in conservative Spain. Dargun, who has written much on this subject,[217] believes that maternal descent was formerly practised among the Germans. He holds further "that the ancient Aryans at the time of their dispersion regarded kinship through the mother as the sole, or chief, basis of blood-kinship, and all their family rights were governed by this principle." There is much conflict of opinion on this matter, and it would, perhaps, be rash to make any definite statement. We may recall what Tacitus says of the Germans:

> The son of a sister is as dear to his uncle as to his father; some even think that the first of these ties is the most sacred and close; and in taking hostages they prefer nephews, as inspiring a stronger attachment, and interesting the family on more sides.

The same authority tells us that the Germans of his day met together to take a clan meal, to settle clan business, *i. e.* for the clan council — and to arrange marriages. This is strong confirmation of what I am trying to establish.[218] Further evidence may be gathered from the ancient religion. There are many Teutonic goddesses, who may well be connected with the primitive tribal-mothers.[219] Religion here, as so often elsewhere, would seem to have been symbolised as feminine. Not only the seers, but the sacrificers among the early Teutons were women.[220] To this evidence may be added that in Germany up to a late period the mother could be the guardian of her children; that a wife had to be bought by the husband, both she and her children remaining under the guardianship of her father. All this points to mother-right and the existence of the maternal clan.[221] Let us note also that in the Slav communities women had the right to vote, and might be elected to the government of the community.

It will interest my readers to know that mother-descent must once have prevailed in Britain. Among the Picts of Scotland kingship was transmitted through women.[222] Bede tells us that down to his own time — the early part of the eighth century — whenever a doubt arose as to the succession, the Picts chose their king from the female rather than from the male line.[223] There is an ancient legend which represents the Irish as giving three hundred wives to the Picts, on the condition that the succession to the crown should always be through their females:

> There were oathes imposed on them,
> By the stars, by the earth,
> That from the nobility of the mother
> Should always be the right to the sovereignty.[224]

Similar traces are found in England: Canute, the Dane, when acknowledged King of England, married Emma, the widow of his predecessor, Ethelred. Ethelbald, King of Kent, married his stepmother, after the death of his father Ethelbert; and, as late as the ninth century, Ethelbald, King of the West Saxons, wedded Judith, the widow of his father. Such marriages are intelligible only if we suppose that the queen had the power of conferring the kingdom upon her consort, which could only happen where maternal descent was, or had been, practised. These marriages with the widow of a king were at one time very common. The familiar example of Hamlet's uncle is one, who, after murdering his brother, married his wife and became king. His acceptance by the people, in spite of his crime, is explained if it was the old Danish custom for marriage with the king's widow to carry the kingdom with it. In Hamlet's position as avenger, and his curious hesitancy, we have really an indication of the conflict between the old and the new ways of descent.[225]

The Celtic population of Britain preserved the institution of the clan much longer than the other European races. In Wales and in Ireland, in particular, communism was strongly established. The clan was responsible for the crimes of its members, paid the fines, and received the compensations.[226] There are numerous indications of mother-right. In Ireland women retained a very high position and much freedom, both before and after marriage, to a late period:

temporary unions were freely allowed, and customs having the force of law safeguarded the rights of the wife. "Every woman," it was said, "is to go the way she willeth freely."[227]

The early Celtic mythologies and folk-records are full of these survivals. Goddesses are frequent as primeval tribal-mothers. Let me give one instance. The Irish goddess Brigit (whose attributes at a later date were transferred to St. Bridget) is referred to in a ninth-century glossary as — *operum atque artificiorum initia*. She was the tribal-mother of the Bringantes. Similarly Vote was tribal-mother of the Burgundians; and the goddess Bil of the Billings, and there are numerous other cases. In a recent book on *Ulster Folklore*,[228] I have been fortunate enough to find a most interesting passage referring to the Irish goddess Brigit. I quote it with pleasure as a fitting ending to this chapter.[229]

> Now, St Bridget had a pagan predecessor, Brigit, a poetess of the Tuatha de Danann, and whom we may perhaps regard as a female Apollo. Cormac in his *Glossary* tells us she was a daughter of the Dagda and a goddess whom all poets adored, and whose sisters were Brigit the physician and Brigit the smith. Probably the three sisters represent the same divine, or semi-divine, person whom we may identify with the British goddess Brigantia and the Gaulish Brigindo.

The Survivals of Mother-Right in Folklore, in Heroic Legends, and in Fairy Stories

IN THE PRECEDING chapter we havefound the former existence of the maternal family, or some indication of it, in the early records of many races, proving this by numerous survivals of customs entirely at variance with the patriarchal conditions. Should it be thought that this claim has not been supported by sufficient evidence, I must plead the difficulties of such an inquiry. My survey has been very incomplete. I am certain, however, that these survivals will be recognised by any one who will undertake for themselves the collection and interpretation of the facts from the records of the past.

There is a point to consider here. The absence, or rather the rarity, of mother-right survivals in some civilisations cannot be counted as proof that the maternal system never existed. As I have shown in the earlier chapters of this book, the mother-age was a transitional stage, between the very early brute-conditions of the family and the second firmly established patriarchate. Now, it is clear that the customs of a transitional stage are very likely to disappear; they are also very likely to be mistaken. Bearing this in mind, the number of survivals that do occur are, I hold, extraordinary, and, indeed, impossible to account for if the maternal family was not a universal stage in the development of society. Moreover, I am certain from my own study that these survivals are of much wider occurrence than is believed, but as yet the facts are insufficiently established.

It now remains to consider a new field of inquiry; and that is the abundant evidence of mother-right to be found in folklore, in heroic legends, and in the fairy-stories of our children. There is a special value in these old-world stories that date back to a time long before written history. They belong to all countries in slightly different forms. We have regarded them as fables, but there was never a fable that did not arise out of truth — not, of course, the outside truth of facts, but from that inward truth of the life and thought of a people, which is what really matters. I cannot, then, do better than conclude the evidence for the mother-age by referring to some few of these myths and legends.

In order to group the great mass of material I will take first the creation myths. One only out of many examples can be given. The Zuñi Indians, who, it will be remembered, are a maternal people, give this account of the beginning of the world. We read how the Sun-god, withdrawing strength from his flesh, impregnated the great waters, until there arose upon them, waxing wide and weighty, the "Fourfold Mother-earth" and the "All-covering Father-sky."

"From the lying together of these twain, upon the great world water, so vitalising, life was conceived, whence began all beings of the earth, men and creatures, in the four-fold womb of the world. Thereupon the Earth-mother repulsed the Sky-father, growing big and sinking deep into the embrace of the waters below, thus separated from the Sky-father, in the embrace of the waters above." The story states, "Warm is the Earth-mother and cold the Sky-father, even as woman is warm and man is cold." Then it goes on, "'So is thy will,' said the Sky-father, 'yet not alone shalt thou helpful be unto our children';" and we learn how the Sky-father assisted the Earth-mother. "Thus in other ways, many diversed, they worked for their offspring."[230]

There is one reflection only I desire to offer on this most beautiful maternal version of the creation legend. Here we find complete understanding of the woman's part; she is the one who gives life; she is the active partner. The Sky-father is represented as her agent, her helper. Why should this be? Contrast this idea with the patriarchal creation story of the Bible.

"And the Lord God said, It is not good that man should be alone; I will make him an help meet for him.... And the Lord God caused a deep sleep to fall upon the man, and he slept; and he took one of his ribs, and closed up the flesh instead thereof: and the rib which the Lord God had taken from the man made he a woman, and brought her unto the man. And the man said, This is now bone of my bones, and flesh of my flesh: she shall be called Woman, because she was taken out of Man."[231]

I would again assert my strong belief that in the religious conception of a people we find the true thoughts and the customs of the period in which they originated. A patriarchal people could not have given expression to a creation myth in which the female idea prevailed, and the mother, and not the father, was dominant. For men have ever fashioned the gods in their own human image, endowing them with their thoughts and actions. The sharp change in the view of woman's part in the relationship of the sexes is clearly symbolised in these creation myths. Yes, it marks the degradation of woman; she has fallen from the maternal conception of the feminine principle, guiding, directing, and using the male, to that of the woman made for the man in the patriarchal Bible story.

Another group of legends that I would notice refer to the conflict between the right of the mother and that of the father in relation to the children. These stories belong to a period of transition. In ancient Greece, as we have seen, the paternal family succeeded the maternal clan. In his *Orestia*, Aeschylus puts in opposition before Pallas Athene the right of the mother and the right of the father. The chorus of the Eumenides, representing the people, defends the position of the mother; Apollo pleads for the father, and ends by declaring, in a fit of patriarchal delirium, that *the child is not of the blood of the mother*. "It is not the mother who begets what is called her child; she is only the nurse of the germ poured into her womb; he who begets is the father. The woman receives the germ merely as guardian, and when it pleases the gods, she preserves it." Plato also brings forward this view, and states that the mother contributes nothing to the child's being. "The mother is to the child what the soil is to the plant; it owes its nourishment to her, but the essence and structure of its nature are derived from the father." Again the Orestes of Euripides takes up the same theory, when he says to Tyndarus: "My father has begotten me, and thy daughter has given birth to me, as the earth receives the seed that another confides to it." Here we trace a different world of thoughts and conceptions; the mother was so little esteemed as to be degraded into the mere nourisher of the child. These patriarchal theories naturally consecrated the slavery of woman.[232]

Another point strikingly illustrated by many of these ancient legends is the struggle for power between the two sexes — a struggle that would seem to have been present at all stages of civilisation, but always most active in periods of transition. One out of many examples is all that I can give. In Hawaii, worship is given to the goddess Pele, the personification of the volcano Kilauea, and the god Tamapua, the personification of the sea, or rather, of the storm which lashes the sea and hurls wave after wave upon the land. The myth tells that Tamapua wooed Pele, who rejected his suit, whereupon he flooded the crater with water, but Pele drank up the water and drove him back into the sea.[233]

Here a brief digression into the early mythologies may be made, although this question of the connection between mother-right and religious ideas is one on which I have already enlarged. The most primitive theogony is that of Mother-Earth and her son. Goddesses are at first of greater importance than gods. The Earth-mother springs from chaos, and in the beginning her children have no father.[234] Traces of such a goddess are to be found in many ancient religions. Afterwards as a modification, or rather a development, of the Earth-mother, we have the goddesses of fertility. This idea arose with the development of agriculture, and was closely connected in the primitive mind with the sex functions. Demeter is of this type; and there are many of these mother-deities who once were universally worshipped. Virgin goddesses are a much later creation, and must be connected with the patriarchal ideals for women. The original god-idea symbolised as woman is the free mother; she is the source of all fertility; she is the goddess of love. The servants of these goddesses were priestesses, or at a later date men dressed as women. At first the gods, in so far as they had any existence, appear in the form of temporary lovers of the goddesses; they are very plainly the transitory male element needful for fertilisation, and then destined to disappear.[235] We find very early the brother as the husband and dependent of the Mother-goddess. Thus Isis did not change or lose her independent position after her marriage to her brother Osiris; her importance as a deity remained always greater than his.[236] Only at a much later stage — the patriarchal stage — was the wandering lover-god or dependent brother-spouse raised to the position of authority of the All-Father. We may find in the religious sexual festivals, common to all civilisations, abundant confirmation of these facts. As one illustration out of many that might be chosen, I will refer to the account given by Prof. K. Pearson[237] of the festival of Sakäçs, held in Babylon in honour of the great goddess Mylitta, who was essentially a mother-goddess of fertility. The festival lasted for five days in the month of July. It was presided over by the priestess of the goddess, who represented the goddess herself. She sat enthroned on a mound which for the time was the sanctuary of the deity, with the altar with oil and incense before her. To her came the god-lover represented by a slave, who made homage and worshipped. From her he received the symbols of kingly power, and she raised him to the throne by her side. As her accepted lover and lord of the festival, he remained for five days, during which the law of the goddess prevailed. Afterwards on the fifth day the god-lover was sacrificed on the pyre. The male element had performed its function.

I cannot leave this subject without emphasising the importance of these erotic-religious festivals, once of universal occurrence. They afford the strongest evidence of the early privileged position of women in the relationships between the two sexes. It is, I think, impossible to avoid giving to this a matriarchal interpretation. For it is by contrasting the religious-sex standpoints of the maternal and the paternal ideals that the inferior position of women under the later system can be demonstrated. Moreover, in much later periods, and even to our own day, we may yet find broken survivals of the old customs. Illustrations are not far to seek in the common festivals of the people in Germany and elsewhere, and as I have myself witnessed them in Spain, a land which has preserved its old customs much more unchanged than is usual.[238] One example may be noted in England, which would seem to have a very ancient origin; it is given by Prof K Pearson.[239] "The Roman *Lupercalia* held on February 15 was essentially a worship of fertility, and the privileges supposed to be attached to women in our own country during this month — especially on February 14 and 29 — are probably fossils of the same sex-freedom."

Passing again to the old legends, we find not a few that attempt to account for both the rise and the decline of the custom of maternal descent. I will give an example of each. Newbold relates that in Menangkabowe, where the female line is observed, it is accounted for by this legend —

> Perpati Sabatang built a magnificent vessel, which he loaded with gold and precious stones so heavily that it got aground on the sands at the foot of the fiery mountains, and resisted the efforts of all the men to get it off. The sages were consulted, and declared that all attempts would be in vain until the vessel had passed over the body of a pregnant woman. It happened that the Rajah's own daughter was in the condition desired; she was called upon to immolate herself for the sake of her country, but refused. At this juncture the pregnant sister of the Rajah boldly stepped forward, and cast herself beneath the prow of the vessel, which instantly put itself in motion, and again

floated on the waves without injury to the princess. Whereupon the Rajah disinherited the offspring of his disobedient daughter in favour of the child of his sister, and caused this to be enrolled in the records of the empire as the law of succession in time to come.[240]

The second illustration is taken from the quarrel between Pallas Athene and Poseidon to which already I have referred. The myth tells us —

> A double wonder sprang out of the earth at the same time — at one place the olive tree and at another water. The people in terror sent to Delphi to ask what should be done. The god answered that the olive tree signified the power of Athene, and the water that of Poseidon; and that it remained with the burgesses to choose after which of the two they would name their town. An assembly was called of the burgesses, both men and women, for it was then the custom to let the women take part in the public councils. The men voted for Poseidon, the women for Athene; and as there were more women than men by one, Athene conquered. Thereupon Poseidon was enraged, and immediately the sea flowed over all the lands of Athens. To appease the sea-god, the burgesses found it necessary to impose a threefold punishment on their wives. They were to lose their votes; the children were to receive no more the mother's name, and they themselves were no longer to be called after the goddess.[241]

The origin of these myths is perfectly clear. There is no reason to force their interpretation by regarding them as historical evidence of a struggle taking place between the maternal and the paternal custom of tracing descent;[242] rather they are poetical explanations, plainly invented to account for women's predominance at a time when such power had come to be considered as unusual. The same may be said of many of these old myths. Man's fancy begins to weave poetic inventions around anything he considers abnormal or is not able to understand. The idea or custom for which an explanation is being sought must, however, have been present for long in the common life and thought of the people. Without realising this, all these old stories become unintelligible. I believe they have been greatly misinterpreted in the thought of writers bound by patriarchal ideas.

The limitation of my space does not allow me to enter into the great amount of evidence provided by these mythical stories of the privileged position of women. One instance, however, may be referred to as an illustration. We find a wide range of stories connected with the mythical Amazons. Now, if I am right, the frequency of these legends among so many races points to the acceptance of the Amazon heroines as an historical fact. Fancy, without doubt, wove the details of their stories, occurrences would be chosen or imagined to give colour to the narratives, but such poetic inventions, with all their repetitions, all their reproductions of what is practically one situation, would take only definite form from conditions so impressed on the popular mind by facts that must have had a real existence. Bearing this in mind, special significance attaches to a discovery recently made by Prof d'Allosso. In the ancient necropolis of Belmonte, dating from the iron age, are two very rich tombs of women warriors with war chariots over their remains. Prof d'Allosso states that several details given by Virgil of the Amazon Camilla, who fought and died on the field of battle, coincide with the details on these tombs. The importance of this discovery is thus very great, as it certainly seems to indicate what I am claiming — that the existence of the Amazon heroines, leaders of armies and sung by the ancient poets, is not a poetic fancy, but an historic reality.[243]

I must turn now to the last group of evidence that I am able to bring forward; to find this we must enter that realm of fancy — the world of fairyland. We shall see that this land has its own customs, and its own laws, entirely at variance with all those to which we are accustomed. How is this to be explained? These stories are founded really on the life of the common people, and they have come down from generation to generation, handed on by the storytellers, from a time long before the day when they were ever collected and written in books. It is the popular and social character of these stories that is so important; they are records of customs and habits long forgotten, but once common in the daily life of the people. In them the past is potent with life, and for this reason they claim the most careful and patient study. I speak of the most familiar stories that we have regarded as foolish fables. Nowhere else can we gain so clear and vivid a picture of the childhood of civilisation, when women were the transmitters of inheritance and the guardians of property.

Let me try to prove this. I have before me a collection of these folk-stories, gathered from many countries. Now, the most popular story (whose theme occurs again and again, the details varied in the different renderings) is concerned with the gaining of a princess as a bride by a wooer, usually of humble birth. This lover to obtain his wife achieves some mighty deed of valour, or performs tasks set for him by the parents of the bride; he thus inherits the kingdom through the daughter of the king. Hans, faring forth to seek his luck; the Dummling in the Golden Goose story; the miller's son, who gained his bride by the wit of his cat, and Aladdin with his magic lamp are well-known examples of this story. The Scottish and Irish legends are particularly rich in examples of these hero lovers. Assipattle, the dirty ash-lad, who wins the fair Gemdelovely and then reigns with her as queen and king, is one of the most interesting. Similar stories may be found in the folklore of every country. Ash-lad figures in many of the Norwegian tales. There is a charming version in the Lapp story of the "Silk Weaver and her husband," where we read, "Once upon a time a poor lad wooed a princess and the girl wanted to marry him, but the Emperor was against the match. Nevertheless she took him at last and they were wed together."[244]

This "fairy theory" of marriage is really the maternal or *beenah* form: such a marriage as was made by Jacob and is still common among all maternal peoples. The inheritance passes through the daughters; the suitors gain their position by some deed of valour or by service done for the bride's family; sometimes it is the mother who sets the task, more often it is the father, while, in some cases, the girl herself imposes the conditions of marriage. It is possible to trace a development in these stories. We can see the growth of purchase-marriage in the service demanded by the parents of the bride, this taking the place of the earlier custom of the bridegroom proving his fitness by some test of strength. Again, those stories in which the arrangement of the marriage remains with the mother or with the girl, and not with the father, must be regarded as the older versions. This change appears also in the conditions of inheritance; in some cases the kingdom passes at once with the bride, in others the half of the kingdom is the marriage portion, while in the later stories the full authority to rule comes only after the death of the king. But always sooner or later the daughter of the king conveys the kingdom to her husband. The sons of the king do not inherit; they are of much less importance than the daughters; they are sent forth to seek their own fortunes. This is the law where the inheritance passes through the daughter.

This law of female inheritance must at one time have been universal. We are brought, indeed, constantly back to that opinion — so amply evidenced by these folk-relics. In the old West country ballad "The Golden Vanity" or "The Lowland's Low," the boy who saves the ship from the Spanish pirate galleon is promised as a reward "silver and gold, with the skipper's pretty little daughter who lives upon the shore." Similarly in the well-known folksong "The Farmer's Boy," the lad who comes weary and lame to the farmer's door, seeking work, eventually marries the farmer's daughter and inherits the farm. Again, Dick Whittington, the poor country lad, who faithfully serves his master in London, marries his employer's daughter. This theme is very frequently found in ballads, romances, and dramas; in all cases the way to fortune for the lover is through marriage — the daughter carries the inheritance.

Let us take Assipattle of the Scottish legend as a type of these hero wooers. He is represented always as the youngest son, held in contempt by his brothers, and merely tolerated by his parents. He lies in the ashes, from which he gains his name. Some emergency arises; a great danger threatens the land or, more often, a princess has to be delivered from a position of peril. Assipattle executes the deed, when his brothers and all others have failed; he frees the land or rescues the king's daughter, and is covered with honour. He marries the princess and inherits the kingdom. Assipattle always begins in the deepest degradation, and ends on the highest summit of glory. There is a special interest in this story. The reader will not have failed to notice the similarity of Assipattle with Cinderella. In both stories the circumstances are the same, only the Ash-lad has been replaced by the Cinder-girl. There is no doubt which version is the older:[245] the one is the maternal form, the other the patriarchal.

The setting of these stories should be noticed. We see the simplicity of the habits and life so vividly represented. All folk-legends deal with country people living near to nature. So similar, indeed, are the customs depicted throughout that these folk-records might well be taken as a picture of the social organisation among many barbarous tribes. I should like to wait to point out these resemblances, such, for instance, as the tendency to personify natural objects, the identification of human beings with animals and trees, found so often in the stories, as well as many other things — the belief in magic and the power of wise women. And what I want to make clear is the very early beginning of these folk-tales; they take us back to the social institutions of the mother-age. Thus there is nothing surprising to find that kingdoms and riches are won by hero-lovers, and that daughters carry the inheritance. This is really what used to happen. It is our individual ideas and patriarchal customs that make these things seem so strange.

I wish I had space in which to follow further these still-speaking relics of a past, whose interest offers such rich reward. In his essay "Ashiepattle, or Hans seeks his Luck" (*The Chances of Death*, Vol II, pp 51-91), Prof. Karl Pearson has fully and beautifully shown the evidence for mother-right to be found in these stories. To this essay the reader, who still is in doubt, is referred. All that has been possible to me is to suggest an inquiry that any one can pursue for himself. It is the difficulty of treating so wide and fascinating a subject in briefest outline that so many things that should be noticed have to be passed over.

The witness afforded by these folk-stories for mother-right cannot be neglected. For what interpretation are we to place on the curious facts they record? Are we to regard this maternal marriage with descent through the daughter, and not the son, as idle inventions of the storytellers? Do these princesses and their peasant wooers belong to the topsy-turvy land of fairies? No: in these stories, drawn from so many various countries, we have echoes of a very distant past. It is by placing the customs here represented by the side of similar social conditions still to be found among primitive maternal peoples, that we find their significance. We then understand that these old, old stories of the folk really take us back to the age in which they first took form. We have read these "fairy stories" to our children, unknowing what they signified — a prophetic succession of witnesses, pointing us back to the ripening of that phase of the communal family, before the establishment of the individual patriarchal rule, when the law was mother-right, and all inheritance was through women.

I would add to this chapter a notice I have just recently lighted on[246] of the ancient warrior, Queen Meave of Ireland. She is represented as tall and beautiful, terrible in her battle chariot, when she drove full speed into the press of fighting men. Her virtues were those of a warlike barbarian king, and she claimed the like large liberty in morals. Her husband was Ailill, the Connaught king; their marriage was literally a partnership wherein Meave, making her own terms, demanded from her husband exact equality of treatment. The three essential qualities on which she insisted were that he should be brave, and generous, and completely devoid of jealousy.

Concluding Remarks

MY INVESTIGATION OF the mother-age might fitly have terminated with the preceding chapter; but the immense interest which attaches to the subject, and the amount of misconception which prevails regarding the origin and conditions of the maternal family, as well as my own special views upon it, induce me to devote a brief final chapter to a few observations that to me seem to be important.

In my little book (which must be regarded rather as a sketch or design than as a finished work) an attempt has been made to approach the problem of the primitive family from a new and decisive standpoint. I am well aware that in certain directions I have crossed the threshold only of the subjects treated. I hope that at least I have opened up suggestions of many questions on which I could not dwell at length. All this may bring the hesitation that leads to further inquiry. And I believe that those of my readers who will follow out an investigation for themselves in any direction — either in the collecting of maternal customs among existing primitive peoples, or in noting the relics of such customs to be met with in historical records and in folklore, will find an ever increasing store of evidence, and that then the discredited mother-age, with its mother-right customs, will become for them what it is for me, a necessary and accepted stage in the evolution of human societies.

Many of the conclusions to which I have come are so completely opposed to those which generally have been accepted as correct, that now, I am at the end of my inquiry it will be well to sum up briefly its result.

The facts I have so rapidly enumerated have a very wide bearing; they serve to destroy the accepted foundations on which the claim for mother-right has hitherto been based. The first stage of the family was patriarchal. All the evidence we possess tends to show that tracing descent through the mother was not the primitive custom. Throughout my aim has been to bring into uniformity the opposing theories of the primeval patriarchate and the maternal family. The current view, so often asserted, and manifestly inspired by a Puritanical ideal, insists that mother-descent arose through uncertain fatherhood, and was connected with an early period of promiscuous relationships between the two sexes. This view has been proved to be entirely wrong. The system of maternal descent was a system framed for order, and had in its origin, at least, no connection with sexual disorder. Further than this, it is certain that marriage in some form has always existed, and that the sexual relationships have never been unregulated. We must renounce any theory of primitive promiscuity. And there is more than this to be said. Such freedom in love and in marriage as we do find in barbarous societies is so strong a proof of friendly feeling and security that it is certain it could not have existed in the first stage of the jealous patriarchate; rather it must have developed at a subsequent period with the growth of the social-tribal spirit, and the liberty of women from the thrall of sexual ownership. In these particulars my opinion differs from all other writers who have sought to establish a theory of matriarchy. I venture to claim that the position of the mother-age has been strengthened, and, as I hope, built up on surer foundations.

Let us cast a brief glance backward over the way that we have travelled.

Our most primitive ancestors, half-men, half-brutes, lived in small, solitary and hostile family groups, held together by a common subjection to the strongest male, who was the father and the owner of all the women, and their children. There was no promiscuity, for there could be no possible union in peace. Here was the most primitive form of jealous ownership by the male, as he killed or drove off his rivals; his fights were the brutal precursors of all sexual restrictions for women. These customs of brute ownership are still in great measure preserved among the least developed races. This explains how there are many rude peoples that exhibit no traces at all of the system of mother-descent. In the lowest nomad bands of savages of the deserts and forests we find still these rough paternal groups, who know no social bonds, but are ruled alone by brute strength and jealous ownership. With them development has been very slow; they have not yet advanced to the social organisation of the maternal clan.

From these first solitary families, grouped submissively around one tyrant-ruler, we reach a second stage out of which order and organisation sprang. In this second stage the family expanded into the larger group of the communal clan. The upward direction of this transformation is evident; the change was from the most selfish individualism to a communism more or less complete — from the primordial patriarchate to a free social organisation, all the members of which are bound together by a strict solidarity of interests. The progress was necessarily slow from the beginning to this first phase of social life. Yet the change came. With the fierce struggle for existence, association was the only possible way, not only to further progress, but to prevent extermination.

It has been shown that the earliest movements towards peace came through the influence of the women, for it was in their interest to consolidate the family, and, by means of union, to establish their own power. Collective motives were more considered by women, not at all because of any higher standard of feminine moral virtue, but because of the peculiar advantages arising to themselves and to their children — advantages of freedom which could not exist in a society inspired by individual inclination. And for this reason the clan system may be considered as a feminine creation, which had special relation to motherhood. Under this influence, the marital rights of the male members were restricted and confined. A system of taboos was established, which as time advanced was greatly strengthened by the sacred totem marks, and became of inexorable strictness. In this way association between the jealous fighting males was made possible.

Here, then, are the reasons that led to the formation of the maternal family and the communal clan. It was a movement that had nothing about it that was exceptional; it was a perfectly natural arrangement — the practical outgrowth of the practical needs of primitive peoples. The strong and certain claim for the acceptance for the mother-age, with its privileged position for women, rests on this foundation.

Let us be quite clear as to the real question involved, for it is a crucial one. I refer to the complete disturbance arising through this change in the family organisation in the relationships between the two sexes. A wife was no longer the husband's property. Her position was unchanged by marriage, for her rights were safeguarded by her kindred, whose own interests could be protected only through her freedom.

If we turn next to the status of men — of the husband and father — in the maternal kindred group, we find their power and influence at first gradually, and then rapidly, decreasing. It was under these conditions of family communism that the rights of the husband and father were restricted on every side. Not only does he not stand out as a principal person from the background of the familial clan; he has not even any recognised social existence in the family group. This restriction of the husband and father was clearly dependent on the form of marriage. We have seen that the individual relationships between the sexes began with the reception of temporary lovers by the woman in her own home. But a relationship thus formed would tend under favourable circumstances to be continued, and, in some cases, perpetuated. The lover became the husband; he left the home of his mother to reside with his wife among her kin; he was still without property or any recognised rights in her clan, with no — or very little — control over the woman and none over her children, occupying, indeed, the position of a more or less permanent guest in her hut or tent. The wife's position and that of her children was assured, and in the case of a separation it was the man who departed, leaving her in possession.

Under such an organisation the family and social customs were in most cases — and always, I believe, in their complete maternal form — favourable to women. Kinship was reckoned through the mother, since in this way alone could the undivided family be maintained. The continuity of the clan thus depending on the women, they were placed in a very special position of importance, the mother was at least the nominal head of the household, shaping the destiny of the clan through the aid of her clan-kindred. Her closest male relation was not her husband, but her brother and her son; she was the conduit by which property passed to and from them. Often women established their own claims and all property was held by them; which under favourable circumstances developed into what may literally be called a matriarchate. In all cases the child's position was dependent entirely on the mother and not on the father. Such a system of inheritance may be briefly summarised as "mother-right."

There is another matter to notice. Every possible experiment in sexual association has been tried, and is still practised among various barbarous races, with very little reference to those moral ideas to which we are accustomed. It is, however, very necessary to remember that monogamy is frequent and indeed usual under the maternal system. We have seen many examples where, with complete freedom of separation held by the wife, lasting and most happy marriages are the rule. When the husband lives with his wife in a dependent position to her family he can do so only in the case of one woman. For this reason polygamy is much less deeply rooted under the conditions in which the communal life is developed than in patriarchal communities. In the complete maternal family it is never common, and is even prohibited.[247]

As we might expect, the case is quite opposite with polyandry. This form of marriage has evident advantages for women when compared with polygamy; it is also a form that requires a certain degree of social civilisation. It clearly involves the limitation of the individual marital rights of the husband. Polyandry in the joint family group was not due to a licentious view of marriage; far otherwise, it was an expression of the communism which is characteristic of this organisation. This fact has been forgotten by many writers, who have regarded this form of the sexual relationships as a very primitive development, connected with group-marriage and promiscuous ownership of women. It is very necessary to be clear on this point. Under the maternal conditions, nothing is more certain than the equality of women with men in all questions of sexual morality. In proof of this it is necessary only to recall the facts we have noted. We find little or no importance attached to virginity, which in itself indicates the absence of any conception of the woman as property. Thus no bride-price is claimed from the husband, who renders service in proof of his fitness as a lover, not to gain possession of the bride. The girl is frequently the wooer, and, in certain cases, she or her mother imposes the conditions of the marriage. After marriage the free provision for divorce (often more favourable to the wife than to the husband) is perhaps of even greater significance. There can, I think, be no doubt that this freedom in love was dependent on the wife's position of security under the maternal form of marriage.

I hold that the facts brought forward entitle us to claim that the maternal communal clan was an organisation in which there was a freer community of interest, far more fellowship in labour and partnership in property, with a resulting liberty for woman, than we find in any patriarchal society. For this reason, shall we, then, look back to this maternal stage as to a golden period, wherein was realised a free social organisation, carrying with it privileges for women, which even today among ourselves have never been established, and only of late claimed? It is a question very difficult to answer, and we must not in any haste rush into mistakes. We found that the mother-age was a transitional stage in the history of the evolution of society, and we have indicated the stages of its gradual decline. It is thus proved to have been a less stable social system than the patriarchate which again succeeded it, or it would not have perished in the struggle with it. Must we conclude from this that the one form of the family is higher than the other — that the superior advantage rests with the patriarchal system? Not at all: rather it proves how difficult is the struggle to socialise. Human nature tends so readily towards individualism; it yields itself up to the joy of possession whenever it is possible.

The impulse to dominate by virtue of strength or property

possession has manifested itself in every age. It cannot be a matter of surprise, therefore, that at this period of social development a rebellion arose against the customs of maternal communism. Within the large and undivided family of the clan the restricted family became gradually re-established by a reassertion of individual interests. In proportion as the family gained in importance (which would arise as the struggle for existence lessened and the need of association was less imperative) the interest of the individual members would become separated from the group to which they belonged. Each one would endeavour to get himself as large a share as possible of what was formerly held in common. As society advanced property would increase in value, and the social and political significance of its possession would also increase. Afterwards, when personal property was acquired, each man would aim at gaining a more exclusive right over his wife and children; he would not willingly submit to the bondage of the maternal form of marriage.

In the earlier days the clan spirit was too strong, now men had shaken off, to a degree sufficient for their purpose, the female yoke, which bound the clan together. We have seen the husband and father moving towards the position of a fully acknowledged legal parent by a system of buying off his wife and her children from their clan-group. The movement arose in the first instance through a property value being connected with women themselves. As soon as the women's kindred found in their women the possibility of gaining worldly goods for themselves, they began to claim service and presents from their lovers. It was in this way for economic reasons, and for no moral considerations that the maternal marriage fell into disfavour. The payment of a bride-price was claimed, and an act of purchase was accounted essential. As we have seen, it was regarded as a condition, not so much of the marriage itself, but of the transference of the wife to the home of the husband and of the children to his kindred. The change was, of course, effected slowly; and often we find the two forms of marriage — the maternal and the purchase-marriage — occurring side by side. What, however, is certain is that the purchase-marriage in the struggle was the one that prevailed.

This reversal in the form of the marriage brought about a

corresponding reversal in the status of women. This is so plain. The women of the family do not now inherit property, but are themselves property, passing from the hands of their father to that of a husband. As purchased wives they are compelled to reside in the husband's house and among his kin, who have no rights or duties in regard to them, and where they are strangers. In a word, the wife occupies the same position of disadvantage as the man had done in the maternal marriage. And her children kept her bound to this alien home in a much closer way than the husband could ever have been bound to her home. The protection of her own kindred was the source of the woman's power and strength. This was now lost. The change was not brought about without a struggle, and for long the old customs contended with the new. But as the patriarchate developed, and men began to gain individual possession of their children by the purchase of their mothers, the father became the dominant power in the family. Little by little individual interests prevailed. Moral limits were set up. Women's freedom was threatened on every side as the jealous ownership, which always arises wherever women are regarded as property, asserted itself. Mother-right passed away, remaining only as a tradition, or preserved in isolated cases among primitive peoples. The patriarchal age, which still endures, succeeded.

Yet in this connection it is very necessary to remember that the reassertion of the patriarchate was as necessary a stage in human development as the maternal stage. Whatever may have been the advantages arising to women from the clan organisation (and that the advantages were great I claim to have proved) such conditions could not remain fixed for ever. For society is not stable; it cannot be, as the need for adjustment is always arising, and at certain stages of development different tendencies are active. No one cause can be isolated, and, therefore, it is necessary in estimating any change to take a synthetic view of many facts that are contemporaneous and interacting. Yet, it would seem that the social and domestic habits of a people are decided largely by the degree of dominance held either by women or men; and almost everything else depends on the accurate adjustment of the rights of the two sexes.

The social clan organised around the mothers carried mankind a long way — a way the length of which we are only beginning to realise. But it could not carry mankind to that family organisation from which so much was afterwards to develop. It was no more possible for society to be built up on mother-right alone than it is possible for it to remain permanently based on father-right.

But there is another aspect of this question that I must briefly touch upon. The opinion that the reversal in the position of authority of the mother and the father arose from male mastery, or was due to any unfair domination on the part of the husband must be set aside. To me the history of the mother-age does not teach this. I believe that the change to the individual family must have been regarded favourably by the women themselves, for such a change could not have arisen, at all events it would not have persisted, if women, with the power they then enjoyed, had not desired it. Nor need this bring any surprise. An arrangement that would give a closer relationship in marriage and the protection of a husband for herself and her children may well have come to be preferred by the wife. Nor do I think it unlikely that she, quite as strongly as the man, may have desired to live apart from her mother and her kindred in her husband's home. Individual interests are not confined to men.

With all the evils father-right has brought to women, we have got to remember that the woman owes the individual relation of the man to herself and her children to the patriarchal system. The father's right in his children (which, unlike the right of the mother, was not founded upon kinship, but rested on the quite different and insecure basis of property) had to be re-established. Without this being done, the family in its complete development was impossible. The survival value of the patriarchal age consists in the additional gain to the children of the father's to the mother's care. I do not think this gain will ever be lost. We women need to remember this lest bitterness stains our sense of justice. It may be that progress could not have been accomplished otherwise; that the cost of love's development has been the enslavement of women. If so, then women will not, in the long account of Nature, have lost in the payment of the price. They may be (when they come again to understand their power) better fitted for their refound freedom.

Such is the history of the past, what is the promise of the future?

We have traced three stages in the past evolution of the family — two individual and patriarchal, one communal and maternal. Is the patriarchal stage, then, the final stage? Has the upward growth, ever yet continuous, been arrested here? The social ideal of the mother-age was a transition and a dream — but as a moment of peace in the records of struggle, following the bloody opening drama in man's history, and then passing into a forgetfulness so complete that its existence by many has been denied. Yet the feet of the race were in the way, though men and women let it pass, blindly unknowing.

Our age is working for scarcely yet formulated changes in the ownership of property and in the status of women. The patriarchal view of woman's subjection to man is being questioned in every direction. What do these movements indicate? If, as seems probable, the individual evolution, already for so long continued, is perishing, what is to take its place? What form will the family take in the future? These are questions to which it is not possible for me here even to attempt to find the answer.[248]

Let us look for a moment in this new direction, the direction of the future, because it is there that the past becomes so important. In our contemporary society there is a deep-lying dissatisfaction with existing conditions, a yearning and restless need for change. We stand in the first rush of a great movement. It is the day of experiments, when again the old customs are in struggle with the new. We are questioning where before we have accepted, and are seeking out new ways in which mankind will go — will go because it must.

Social institutions alter very slowly as a rule; for long a change may pass unnoticed, until one day it is discovered that a step forward has been taken. Those changes that appear so new and are bringing fear to many today, are but the last consequences of causes that for long have been operating slowly. The extraordinary enthusiasm now sweeping through womanhood reveals behind its immediate feverish expression a great power of emotional and spiritual initiative. Wide and radically sweeping are the changes in women's outlook. So much stronger is the promise of a vital force when they have refound their emancipation. To this end women must gain economic security, and the freedom for the full expression of their womanhood. The ultimate goal I conceive — at least I hope — is the right to be women, not the right to become like men. There can be no gain for women except this. To be mothers were women created and to be fathers men. This rightly considered is the deepest of all truths.

What is needed at present is that women should be allowed to rediscover for themselves what is their woman's work, rather than that they should continue to accept perforce the role which men (rightly or wrongly) have at various times allowed to them throughout the patriarchal ages. This necessity is as much a necessity for men as it is for women.

I do not think that women will fail (even if for a time they stumble a little) in finding the way. The vital germinal spot of each forward step in women's position must be sought with the women who are the conscious mothers of the race. The great women reformers are not those who would have women act just like men in all externals, but those who are conscious that all men are born of women. In this lies women's strength in the past and in this must be their strength in that glad future that is to be. But only if motherhood is regarded as an intrinsic glory, and children are born in freedom. Think what this means. The birth of a child, in so far as its mother has not received the sanction of a man, is subject to the fire and brimstone of public scorn. And this scorn is the most pitiful result in all the patriarchal record. A woman's natural right is her right to be a mother, and it is the most inglorious page in the history of woman that too often she has allowed herself to be deprived of that right. Women have this lesson first to learn. We, and not men, must fix the standard in sex, for we have to play the chief part in the racial life. Let us, then, reacquire our proud instinctive consciousness, which we are fully justified in having, of being the mothers of humanity; and having that consciousness, once more we shall be invincible.

Notes & References

1) The *Mahâbhârata.* The Great God thus addresses Shakti, when he asks her to describe the duties of women I quote from a pamphlet by Dr Ananda Coomaraswamy: *Sati: A Vindication of the Hindu Woman..*
2) McGee: "The Beginning of Marriage," *American Anthropologist,* Vol IV, p 378.
3) Westermarck, "The Position of Women in Early Civilisations," *Sociological Papers,* 1904.
4) For instance, Maine (*Early Law and Custom*), in speaking of tribes who still trace their descent from a single ancestress, says, "The outlines" (*i. e.* of the maternal family) "may still be marked out, *if it be worth any one's while to trace it.*"
5) This book was mentioned to me in a letter from Mr H G Wells.
6) *Das Mutterrecht* was published in Stuttgart in 1861.
7) *Primitive Marriage,* published 1865 *Studies in Ancient History,* which includes a reprint of *Primitive Marriage;* first edition 1876, second edition 1886. *The Patriarchal Theory,* a criticism of this theory, is based on the papers of Mr McLennan and edited by his brother.
8) Prof Giraud-Teulon's *La Mère chez certains Peuples de l'Antiquité* is founded on the introduction to *Das Mutterrecht.* This little book of fascinating reading is the best and easiest way of studying Bachofen's theory.
9) *Das Mutterrecht,* Intro, p xiii.
10) *Das Mutterrecht,* Intro, p vii.
11) *Ibid,* Intro, p xv.
12) *Das Mutterrecht,* Intro, p xxiv and p 10.
13) *Ibid,* Intro, p xiv.
14) *Ibid,* Intro, p xv.
15) *Das Mutterrecht,* p 18.
16) I have taken much of this passage from Mr McLennan's criticism of Bachofen's theory, *Studies in Ancient History,* pp 319-25.
17) *Das Mutterrecht,* Intro, pp vii-viii.
18) *Das Mutterrecht,* pp 18-19.
19) *The History of Human Marriage,* p 105.
20) *Das Mutterrecht,* p 85.
21) *Das Mutterrecht,* pp 73, 85. Compare also McLennan, *Studies,* p 322, and Starcke, *The Primitive Family in Its Origin and Development.*

22) *Ibid*, p 85.
23) *Das Mutterrecht*, Intro, p xxvii.
24) *Ibid*, Intro, p xxix.
25) *Studies in Ancient History*, pp 83, *et seq.*
26) *History of Human Marriage*, pp 51-133 It is on this question that my own opinion has been changed, compare *The Truth about Woman*, p 120.
27) See next chapter on the Patriarchal Theory.
28) Starcke, *The Primitive Family in its Origin and Development*, pp 36-37.
29) The reader is referred to *The Truth about Woman*, pp 87-114. In the courtships and perfect love marriages of many birds we find jealous combats replaced by the peaceful charming of the female by the male.
30) Darwin, *Descent of Man*, Wallace, *The Malay Archipelago*, and Brehm, *Thierleben*
31) *Social Origins and Primal Law*, pp 4, 21 Westermarck, pp 13, 42, *Primal Law*, pp 209-12.
32) *Social Origins and Primal Law*, p 230. Mr Atkinson writes this to show that there can be no connection between these groups of young males and the polyandrous marriages of Mr McLennan's theory. The first italics in the passage are his own; the second are mine. Why I wish to emphasise this point will soon be seen I have already mentioned how I was recommended to read *Social Origins* to convince me of my mistake in accepting the mother-age. It has done just the opposite, and has given me the clue to many difficulties that I was before unable to clear up. This is why I am following this book rather than other authorities in my examination of the patriarchal theory. I take this opportunity of recording my debt to the authors, and of expressing my thanks to Mr Wells, who recommended me to read the book.
33) *Primal Law*, pp 231-32.
34) *Studies*, Chap VII: "Exogamy: Its Origin."
35) *History of Human Marriage*, Chap XIV: "Prohibition of Marriage between Kindred."
36) *Mystic Rose.*
37) *Primal Law*. The Chapter "From the Group to the Tribe," pp 250-63.
38) Mr Atkinson refers to these clandestine marriages. He does not, however, connect the custom, as I suggest, with any action on the part of the young women.
39) *Primal Law*, p 256.
40) *The Mystic Rose*, pp 460-61.
41) This is the number given by Prof Tylor "The Matriarchal Family System," *Nineteenth Century*, July 1896.
42) *History of Human Marriage*, pp 97-104.
43) "The Position of Woman in Early Civilisations," *Sociological Papers*, 1904.
44) Morgan, *Houses and House-Life of the American Aborigines*, p 64.
45) Tylor, "The Matriarchal Family System," *Nineteenth Century*, July 1896.
46) McLennan, *The Patriarchal Theory*, p 208 Heriot, *Travels through the Canadas*, p 323.
47) The reader is referred to Morgan's interesting *Houses and House-Life of the Aborigines* It is from this work that many of the facts I give have been taken.

48) Morgan, *Ancient Society,* p 62. Also *Houses and House-Life of the American Aborigines.*
49) *Historical and Statistical Information Respecting the History, Condition, and Prospects of the Indian Tribes of the United States,* in 6 voumels, Vol III, p 195. See also *Notes on the Iroquois* and *The Indian in his Wigwam.*
50) Heriot, *op cit,* pp 321-22.
51) *Houses and House-Life of American Aborigines,* pp 65-66.
52) Morgan, *League of the Iroquois,* p 324; Heriot, *op cit,* pp 323, 329; Schoolcraft, *op cit,* Vol III, p 191.
53) Heriot, pp 231-37. See also Report of an Official of Indian Affairs on two of the Iroquoian tribes, cited by Hartland *Primitive Paternity,* Vol I, p 298.
54) *Charleroix,* Vol V, p 48, quoted by Hartland, *op cit,* Vol II, p 66.
55) Powell, *Rep Bur Ethn,* I, 63.
56) Owen: *Musquakie Indians,* p 72.
57) I have summarised the account of the Wyandot government as given by Hartland, who quotes from Powell's "Wyandot Government," *First Annual Report of the Bureau of American Ethnology,* 1879-1880, pp 61ff.
58) *The Native Races of the Pacific States of South America,* 5 vols, Vol I, p 555. See also Morgan.
59) Schoolcraft, *Indian Tribes,* p 262, gives an account of these houses. A similar plan of living is reported of the Maya Indians.
60) Bancroft, *op cit,* pp 546-47.
61) Heriot, *op cit,* p 340.
62) Cushing, "My Visit to the Zuñi Indians," *Century Magazine,* 1883. Prof Tylor gives these passages in his account of the Zuñi Indians, "The Patriarchal Family System," *Nineteenth Century,* 1896. I have quoted from him.
63) Mrs Stevenson, in the *Report Bureau Ethnological,* XXIII, pp 290-93.
64) Voth, *Traditions of the Hopi,* pp 67, 96, 133 *Rep Bur Ethn,* XIII, 340 Hartland, *Primitive Paternity,* Vol II, pp 74-76.
65) *Rep Bur Ethn* IX, p 19. Hartland, *Ibid,* pp 76-77.
66) Bancroft, *op cit,* Vol I, p 549.
67) Bancroft, *op cit,* Vol I, p 277; Power's *Tribes of California,* pp 22, 56.
68) Bancroft, *op cit,* Vol II, p 685.
69) *History of Human Marriage,* p 500.
70) Azara, *Voyages dans l'Amérique Méridionale,* Vol II, p 93.
71) Bancroft, *op cit,* Vol I, pp 661-62.
72) "The Beginning of Marriage," *American Anthropologist,* Vol IX, p 376. Also *Rep Bur Ethn,* XVII, 275.
73) In an Introduction to *The Khasis,* by P R Gurdon. This work, written by one who had a long and intimate knowledge of the Khasi tribes, gives an admirable account of the people, their institutions and domestic life. See also Sir J Hooker, *Himalayan Journal,* Vol II, pp 273 *et seq;* Dalton, *Descriptive Ethnology of Bengal;* and a series of papers by J R Logan, in the *Journal of the Indian Archipelago,* 1850-57. Mr Frazer (*The Golden Bough,* Part IV, *Adonis, Attis, Osiris,* p 387) gives a short account of the Khasis; also McGee in the article *The Beginning of Marriage* already quoted.
74) *The Khasis,* pp 62, 64, 82. All the facts I have given of the Khasis are taken from Mr Gurdon's work, unless otherwise stated.

75) An incantation used in addressing this god begins: "O Father, *Thaulang,* who hast enabled me to be born, who hast given me my stature and my life" This is very certain proof that the maternal system among the Khasis has no connection with uncertainty of paternity.
76) This is the opinion of Sir Charles Lyell and Mr Gurdon. We may compare the remark of Prof Karl Pearson: "According to the evidence not only the seers but the sacrificers among the early Teutons were women."
77) Fischer, *Tour As Soc,* Bengal, Vol IX, Part II, p 834.
78) Dalton, *Descriptive Ethnology of Bengal,* p 57.
79) McGee, *The Beginning of Marriage.*
80) *The Khasis,* p 81.
81) Mrs Chapman Catt has an article in the April number of *Harper's Magazine* on "A Survival of Matriarchy." It gives an account of her visit to the Malay States, and the favourable position of the women under the maternal customs. I have received a letter from the great American champion of Women's Rights in which she states how pleased she is that I am writing this book on the Mother-age. "There are many facts," she says, "of the early power of women which the great world does not know."
82) *Marriage and Kinship in Early Arabia,* p 74. See also Marsden, *History of Sumatra,* p 225.
83) "The Beginning of Marriage," *American Anthropologist,* Vol IX, p 376.
84) *Lettres edefiantes et curieux,* Vol XVIII, p 441, copied in Dunhalde, *Description de la Clune,* Vol I, p 166, and cited by McGee.
85) Dalton, *Descriptive Ethnology of Bengal,* pp 64, 142. See also Tylor, "The Matriarchal Theory," *Nineteenth Century,* July 1896, p 89.
86) Moore, *Marriage Customs: Modes of Courtship,* etc, p 261 Rengger, *Naturgeschichte der Säugelliere von Paraguay,* p 11, cited by Westermarck, *op cit,* p 158.
87) J M Wheeler, "Primitive Marriage," an article in *Progress,* 1885, p 128.
88) McGee, "The Beginning of Marriage," *American Anthropologist,* Vol IX.
89) Haddon, "Western Tribes of the Torres States," *Journal of the Anthropological Society,* Vol XIX, February 1890, Cited by Havelock Ellis, *Psychology of Sex,* Vol III, p 185.
90) For further examination of this question of the supposed passivity of the woman in courtship, see *The Truth about Woman,* pp 65-69, 251-57.
91) *Die socialen Einrichtungen der Pelauer Die Religion, de Pelauer.* Mr Frazer, *Golden Bough,* Part IV, *Adonis, Attis, Osiris,* pp 387 *et seq,* summarises the account of Kubary. See also Waitz-Gerland, Vol V, Part II, p 106 *et seq,* and an account of the Pelews given by Ymer.
92) Semper, *Die Palau-Inseln,* p 68, cited by Westermarck *op cit,* p 211.
93) Ymer, Vol IV, p 333.
94) Frazer, *op cit,* p 380.
95) Hodgson, *Journal of Asiatic Society of Bengal,* 1847 (Dalton).
96) Duveyrier, *Toûareg du Nord,* p 337 *et seq.*
97) Chavanne, *Die Sahara,* pp 181, 209, 234.
98) *Ibid,* p 387.
99) Duveyrier, *op cit,* p 430.
100) *Ibid,* p 362.
101) *Ibid,* p 347.

102) Chavanne, *op cit,* p 208 *et seq.*
103) Duveyrier, *op cit,* p 429.
104) Letourneau, *The Evolution of Marriage,* pp 180-81.
105) *See* Westermarck, *op cit,* pp 54-56.
106) Starcke's *Primitive Family,* pp 85-88; Letourneau, *Evolution of Marriage,* pp 80-81, 311-312; Hartland, *Primitive Paternity,* Vol I, pp 269, 288.
107) Alice Werner, "Our Subject Races", *National Reformer,* Aug 1897, p 169.
108) *Travels,* p 109.
109) Lippert, *Kulturgeschichte,* etc, Vol II, p 57; Hartland, *Primitive Paternity,* Vol I, pp 274, 286.
110) Letourneau, pp 306-307; citing Laing, *Travels in Western Africa.*
111) Giraud-Teulon, *Les origines du mariage et de la famille,* pp 215 *et seq.*
112) Hodgson, *Journal of Asiatic Society of Bengal,* 1855, Vol XVIII, p 707, cited by Starcke, *op cit,* pp 79, 285.
113) Hartland, *op cit,* Vol II, pp 155-57.
114) This custom prevails, for instance, among the Kharwars and Parahiya tribes, and is common among the Ghasiyas, and is also practised among the Tipperah of Bengal.
115) *Kinship and Marriage in Early Arabia* See also Barton, *Semitic Origins.*
116) *Academy,* March 27, 1886.
117) Spencer, *Descriptive Sociology,* Vol V, p 8, citing Petherick, *Egypt, the Sudan, and Central Africa,* pp 140-41.
118) Thomas, *Sex and Society,* pp 73-74, quoting Waitz-Gerland.
119) McLennan, *The Patriarchal Theory,* p 235.
120) Marsden, *History of Sumatra,* pp 225-27.
121) Forbes, *Eleven Years in Ceylon,* Vol I, p 333.
122) Macdonald, *Africana,* Vol I, p 136.
123) Livingstone, *Travels,* p 622.
124) Riedel, p 205; cited by McLennan, *Patriarchal Theory,* p 326.
125) *Journal Asiatic Society of Bengal,* Vol IX, p 603.
126) Bancroft, Vol I, p 549.
127) *Journal African Society,* VIII, 15 *et seq.*
128) Torday and Joyce, *J A I,* XXXV, 410.
129) McLennan, *The Patriarchal Theory,* pp 324-25, 240.
130) Dennett, *Jour Afr Soc,* I, 266.
131) *Jour Afr Soc,* I, 412.
132) Hartland, *Primitive Paternity,* Vol I, pp 275 *et seq.*
133) *Old New Zealand,* p 110.
134) McLennan, *The Patriarchal Theory.*
135) *Survey of Canada,* Report for 1878-79, 134 B; cited by Frazer, *Totemism,* p 76.
136) Turner, *Samoa,* p 78.
137) *Das Mutterrecht,* p 20, quoted by Starcke, *op cit,* pp 126-27.
138) Wilken, *Das Matriarchat bei den alten Arabern,* p 26.
139) Wilken, *op cit,* p 26.
140) Wade, *Journal Asiatic Society of Bengal,* Vol VI, p 196.
141) See *Truth about Woman,* pp 160-161, for account of Madagascar.
142) *Journal Asiatic Society of Bengal,* Vol IX, p 603.
143) This passage is quoted from *The Truth about Woman,* p 171. I give it here, because its importance seems to me to be very great.

144) *Daily Life and Origin of the Tasmanians,* p 55.
145) Everard im Thurn, *Among the Indians of Guiana.*
146) Macdonald, "East Central African Customs," *Journal Anthropological Institute,* February 1890, p 342.
147) *Journal Anthropological Institute,* February 1890, p 342.
148) Owen, *Transactions of the Ethnological Society,* New Series, Vol II, p 36.
149) Mason, *Woman's Share in Primitive Culture,* p 143.
150) Turner, *Nineteen Years in Polynesia,* p 424.
151) *Life and Adventures of William Buckley,* p 43.
152) *Journal Anthropological Institute,* Aug 1890, p 61.
153) *Australian Races,* cited by Ellis, *Man and Woman,* p 9 note.
154) Haydes and Deniker, *Mission Scientifique de Cape Horn,* Vol VII, 1891.
155) *Journal of the Anthropological Institute,* February 1892, p 307.
156) Warburton Pike, *Barren Grounds,* p 75.
157) Havelock Ellis, *Man and Woman,* p 5.
158) *A Journey from Prince of Wales's Fort to the Northern Ocean,* p 55.
159) Mason, *op cit,* p 10.
160) Im Thurn, *Among the Indians of British Guiana.*
161) Macdonald, *Journal Anthropological Institute,* August 1892.
162) *Kamilaroi and Kurnai,* pp 133, 147.
163) Cited by Ellis, *Man and Woman,* p 4.
164) H H Johnston, *The Kilimanjaro Expedition*; Parke, *Experiences in Equatorial Africa.* These examples are cited by Ellis.
165) "The Beginnings of Agriculture," *American Anthropologist,* Oct 1895, p 37.
166) Thomas, *Sex and Society,* p 136.
167) Mason, *op cit* p 24.
168) *Cont North American Ethnology,* Vol III, p 167.
169) Mrs Bishop, *Journeys in Persia and Kurdistan,* cited by H Ellis, *op cit,* p 6.
170) *Jour Anthrop Inst,* Vol I, p 190.
171) "Magic Songs of the Finns," *Folklore,* March 1892.
172) *American Antiquarian,* January 1899.
173) "Our Subject Races," *The Reformer,* April 1897, p 43.
174) *Journal Anthropological Institute,* May 1892, p 427, cited by H Ellis.
175) *Kamilaroi and Kurnai,* p 358.
176) Ratzel, *History of Mankind,* Vol II, p 130.
177) Robertson Smith, *Kinship and Marriage in Early Arabia,* p 65.
178) Hoffman, "The Menomini Indians," *Fourteenth Report of the Bureau of American Ethnology,* p 288.
179) Papers of the *Archaeological Institute of America,* Vol II, p 138.
180) Herodotus, Book II, p 35.
181) Starcke, *The Primitive Family,* p 67.
182) Diodorus, Book I, p 27.
183) For a fuller account of the position of women in Egypt, see the chapter on this subject in *The Truth about Woman,* pp 179-201.
184) H Ellis, *Psychology of Sex,* Vol VI, p 393.
185) Letourneau, *Evolution of Marriage,* p 335.
186) *Golden Bough,* Part I; *The Magic Art,* Vol II, pp 270, 289, 312.
187) Müller and Bachofen, cited by Giraud-Teulon, *op cit,* pp 283-84.

188) *The Truth about Woman*, pp 227-42.
189) Grote, *History of Greece*, Vol III, p 95.
190) Letourneau, *op cit* pp 335-36.
191) Herodotus, Book I, p 172.
192) See pp 129-31, also *The Truth about Woman*, pp 199-201.
193) Gladstone, *Homeric Studies*, Vol II, p 507; Donaldson, *Woman*, pp 18-19.
194) McLennan, "Kinship in Ancient Greece"; Essay in *Studies in Ancient History*, pp 195-246
195) Plutarch, *Apophthegms of the Lacedaemonians*, LXV.
196) Pausanias, III, 20 (10), (Frazer's translation).
197) Herodotus, III, 119.
198) Sophocles, *Antigone*, line 905 *et seq*.
199) *Iliad*, VI, 429-30.
200) *The Truth about Woman*, pp 210-27.
201) Gen xxx, 18-30; xxxi, 14, 41.
202) Gen xxxi, 43.
203) Gen xxiv, 5, 53.
204) Judges xv, 1.
205) Numb, xxxii, 8-11. See Letourneau, *Evolution of Marriage*, p 326.
206) Gen xxiii, 13.
207) Numb xxxvi, 4-8.
208) Gen xii, 10-20.
209) 2 Sam xiii, 13-16 and 37.
210) Exod vi, 20.
211) Gen xi 26-29.
212) See pp 156-61.
213) Letourneau, *op cit* 328.
214) See in this connection my book, *Spain Revisited*, pp 291-304.
215) See pp 107-09.
216) *Spain Revisited; Things Seen in Spain; Moorish Cities.*
217) *Mutterrecht und Raubehe und ihre Reste im Germanischen Recht und Leben*, Vol XVI, quoted by Starcke, *The Primitive Family*, pp 103 *et seq*.
218) *De moribus Germanorum*, XX. See also K Pearson, *The Chances of Death*, Vol II, p 132.
219) Grimm, *Mythologie*, Vol I, p 248.
220) K Pearson, *The Chances of Death*, Vol II, p 102.
221) Starcke, *op cit* p 105, citing Dargun and Grimm. See also Letourneau, *op cit* pp 339-40.
222) Giraud-Teulon, *op cit*, pp 41-42.
223) Bede, II, 1-7.
224) McLennan, *Studies*, p 46.
225) See Frazer, *Golden Bough*, Part I; *The Magic Art*, Vol II, 282-83.
226) Letourneau, *op cit*, p 338; Maine, *Early Institutions*, pp 113 *et seq*.
227) Rhys and Brynmor-Jones, *The Welsh People*.
228) By E Andrews, p 18.
229) I would refer the reader to a most interesting article on "Old English Clans" (*Cornhill*, Sept 1881); this I had not read when I wrote this chapter. The author holds that the clan system was once common to the whole Aryan race. In the Teutonic stock its memory died out in an early stage of

development, owing to the strong individuality of the Teutonic mind. Yet it has left behind it many traces Numerous examples are given. Perhaps the most interesting is the evidence showing that totemism seems to have existed; the clan names being taken from animals or plants.

230) Cushing, *Zuñi Creation Myths.*

231) Gen ii, 18, 21-23.

232) McLennan, *Studies,* "Kinship in Ancient Greece"; Letourneau, *Evolution of Marriage,* pp 336-337, and Starcke, *The Primitive Family,* pp 115-16.

233) Starcke, pp 249-250, citing Bachofen's *Antiquarische Briefe,* Vol I, p 140.

234) K Pearson, *Chances of Death,* Vol II: Essays on the Mother-age Civilisation, etc. Many of the facts given in this chapter are taken from these illuminative essays.

235) K Pearson, *Ibid,* p 102.

236) *The Truth about Woman,* p 198.

237) *Ibid,* pp 109-10.

238) See *Spain Revisited,* and *Things Seen in Spain.*

239) *Ibid,* p 158.

240) Newbold, *Account of the British Settlements in the Straits of Malacca,* Vol II, p 221.

241) McLennan, *Studies,* "Kinship in Ancient Greece," p 235.

242) This is done by Bachofen, and also, to some extent, by McLennan.

243) See *The Truth about Woman,* p 228.

244) K Pearson, *The Truth about Woman,* p 70 note.

245) In this connection, see K Pearson in the essay already quoted, p 85 *et seq.*

246) "Ancient Irish Sagas," *Century,* Jan 1907.

247) It is significant that in Sumatra polygamy occurs with the *djudur* marriages, where the wife is bought and lives with her husband, while it is unknown in the maternal marriages It is frequent in Africa and elsewhere, when the marriage is not the maternal form.

248) I hope to do so in a future book on *Motherhood.*